CORK G

with John O'Shea

PUBLISHED BY HERO BOOKS
1 WOODVILLE GREEN
LUCAN
CO. DUBLIN
IRELAND

Hero Books is an imprint of Umbrella Publishing
First Published 2022
Copyright © John O'Shea 2022
All rights reserved

A CIP record for this book is available from the British Library

ISBN 9781910827550

Cover design and formatting: jessica@viitaladesign.com

Photographs: Sportsfile

★ DEDICATION ★

To all the players who have worn the Cork City jersey

★ CONTENTS ★

★ ACKNOWLEDGEMENTS ★

SINCE I FIRST started attending matches in Turner's Cross in the summer of 2004, heading off to watch Cork City FC games has been a weekly date in my diary.

In more recent years, I have had the pleasure of covering this great club, and League of Ireland football generally, in my profession as a football journalist. To the players of Cork City FC, this book well and truly is yours.

My primary objective in undertaking this project was to share some of the memories and stories from City players right across the years. I will always appreciate the time you all afforded me in this endeavour.

Undertaking something like this and reflecting on the big nights in the history of Cork City, it once again illustrates just how great a football club this is. All going well, there will be many more rich memories and more stories to be excitedly recalled by the current and future generations of City players over the years to come.

I must say an absolutely huge thank you to Liam Hayes of Hero Books. Right from the very outset, Liam has been an excellent source of support and an absolute pleasure to deal with as an editor and publisher.

As I have already said, I have had the privilege of being able to combine both of my passions, sports and writing, in recent years and I would like to extend a special thanks to *The Echo* sports editor John McHale, who gave me my first opportunity in sports journalism and has allowed me to write regularly for the newspaper and also online. This is something which I will always appreciate and will be forever grateful for. A further thanks to everyone in the sports department at *The Echo*, especially deputy sports editor Éamonn Murphy, Rory Noonan, Noel O'Sullivan and Mark Woods for all your help.

Also, a massive thank you to Noel Spillane who has been a great mentor and a friend over the years. A special mention also to Ruairí O'Hagan, Denis Hurley, Trevor Welch, Kieran McCarthy, Ger McCarthy and David Byrne for their assistance and advice throughout the process of building this book.

From Cork City FC, I cannot thank Éanna Buckley enough for his help and providing me with numerous contact numbers of City players from various different eras.

And, most importantly, to my family, thank you! Words cannot describe how grateful I am for your constant support and encouragement.

John O'Shea
August 2022

PHILIP LONG

BRAY WANDERERS 0 ★ CORK CITY 1
FAI CUP SEMI-FINAL (1-1 on aggregate)
Carlisle Grounds
APRIL 16, 1989

Philip Long in action against Bohemians at Dalymount Park in 1998

★ **BRAY WANDERERS:** J Moran; T McKeever, M Doohan, C Phillips, B Cosgrove, M Nugent, D Judge, A Cairns, E Davis, A Smith, J Ryan.

★ **CORK CITY:** P Harrington; P Bowdren, N Healy, B Carey, **P Long**, P Freyne, M Conroy, D Barry, L Murphy, J Caulfield, K Nugent. Subs: P Duggan for Bowdren, K Nagle for Duggan.

THE ACTION

A GOAL, COURTESY of Philip Long from the penalty spot took the FAI Cup tie between Bray Wanderers and the Leesiders to a replay.

City, who showed a significant improvement from their first leg display, took the tie into a third match for the right to face Derry City in the final.

Bray went close to finding the back of the net on 32 minutes, when Martin Nugent's corner was headed on by Alan Smith at the near post. But Mick Doohan saw his attempt cleared off the line by City's Patsy Freyne.

The breakthrough for City arrived on 39 minutes when Dave Barry was taken down by a tackle from Dermot Judge. Up stepped Long, and he slotted home the subsequent spot kick courtesy of a low powerful drive.

Cork's best spell in the game came during the second-half. John Caulfield went close on 65 minutes with a diving header. And City were denied a late match winner on aggregate when Barry smashed a tremendous volley off the underside of the crossbar with Bray goalkeeper Moran well beaten.

The 1988/89 FAI Cup was the only time that the semi-finals were played over two legs. In the first leg at Turner's Cross, Bray recorded a 1-0 win with Eugene Davis hitting the net. After City won the second leg 1-0 at the Carlisle Grounds, the Leesiders then subsequently won the replay 4-0 at Turner's Cross a few days later.

★★★★★

"

WE WERE UNDER pressure after the first game, but to be honest, we didn't fear Bray and we thought we would beat them.

But when they came down and played us in Turner's Cross, which was a fortress really and they beat us 1-0, we got a bit worried. We were going back to their patch and trying to beat them up there. It wasn't going to be easy.

We got the penalty, and I stuck it away.

That is the game that really sticks out for me because of the pressure of that particular day. Even when we were going home on the bus and we realised what we were after doing, we knew we would beat them at Turner's Cross on the Wednesday.

We didn't think we'd beat them 4-0, but we knew we were going to beat them. The first game was an eye-opener because we didn't think that they would take us. So that particular game, and series of games, sticks out in my head. I played a lot of games for Cork City down through the years and I'd forget ninty percent of them, to be honest.

But that Bray game always sticks out for me. The FAI Cup that particular year, you had a home and away legs when you got to the semi-final. A lot of teams feared coming to Cork City.

The first game, we were without Dave Barry, who was playing gaelic football with Cork at the time; that was a little bit of a bonus for Bray, because without doubt Dave would have been the best midfielder in the country at the time.

We went up to Bray and it was pressuring the whole way. Kevin Nugent was on loan from Leyton Orient, and he was up front with John Caulfield. In the last 10 minutes, he got pulled down for a penalty. I used to take the penalties at the time.

I remember getting the ball and walking into the box, just looking around and kind of delaying taking the penalty a little bit. Kind of psyching out the goalkeeper a little bit.

I was looking at the lads around me and they were staring at me... as much as to say... *there is a bit of pressure here and you'll have to put it away.*

So, I put the ball down anyway. When I turned around and faced back down the pitch, I could see Liam Murphy in the distance... and Liam Murphy would never watch a penalty. He was our club captain at the time. He had his head in his hands.

He turned around and just didn't want to look.

I scored the penalty... it was 1-1 then on aggregate. The game went into extra-time, and it finished 1-1, which meant there had to be a toss-up of where to play the deciding game, whether it was back in Bray or down at Turner's Cross.

The last 15 minutes of that game we had one of our players go off injured, he was carried off... Pat Duggan. So, we didn't know if he would be available for the next game.

Phil Harrington then on the way up told us that he's going away after the game for a family reunion back to Wales... he'd be gone for the week. So, there was more pressure there. I think the Saturday before the game as well, the Hillsborough disaster occurred.

So, there was a lot of things happening at that particular time. Phil Harrington was getting onto Liam Murphy to see if we won the toss, because it was easier for him to come back to Wales through Dublin port than going down to Turner's Cross.

We won the toss and of course we chose to play at home. A couple of hours before kick-off, Phil was due back down in the train station. At that time the train stopped in Limerick Junction, and you'd get off there to come to Cork.

Phil didn't get off and he ended up down towards Killarney direction. So, he was a little bit delayed getting to the ground. That was a bit nerve wracking.

We ended up beating Bray 4-0. It was just an unbelievable performance from the players... and that is the game that really stands out. We went on to then play in the FAI Cup final against Derry City. We lost that final after a replay. Dave Barry hit the post in the first game... Felix Healy scored the Derry City goal in the replay.

It was a very exciting time to play for Cork City. When Derry City won the cup and we qualified for Europe, we went off to play Torpedo Moscow, which was another exiting tie.

It was something that none of us were accustomed to. All for just playing football with Cork City. So, it was the start of a very, *very* big, and long story... it really was a brilliant time.

Noel O'Mahony knew how to talk to the players, and he knew what we had to do. He played with Cork Hibs in earlier years, so he knew what it was like to defend. Were we a defensive team? We were, because he didn't know any better really, as such. We were solid, but he gave players the chance to express themselves too. The likes of Patsy (Freyne) and Dave Barry… John Caulfield up front, just give them the ball was his attitude.

We'd win the ball and just leave them to play with it. In those particular times when a defender got the ball, he just moved it forward… you'd never see the ball going backwards, unless it was back to the 'keeper, if you were caught. Whereas nowadays, the ball is going backwards all of the time.

It was different times. Every time I got the ball, I was always told either give it to Patsy or Davy or send it up front. That was no problem, and it was my job to just win the ball and give it to others. By hook or by crook, you had to win it. That was drilled into us. That was just the way football was played at the time.

I mean, when you wore the jersey there was fierce pride… that is what it was. I still have my original jersey. You got a couple of bob for playing, but that would just take you out on a night for a couple of drinks.

It was just sheer pride with ninty percent of us really. We just played for the enjoyment of the game. Very seldom then you'd be out with injuries, because you'd always want to come back… you didn't want to let anyone down. There were no such things as hamstrings or groins or anything in the early years.

You didn't know what they were… you had a pain in your leg and that was it. If you could play, you played… if you can't, then so be it, it was as simple as that.

It was a great team, and it was all locals. I think we only had about three pros who came in. You had Mick Conroy who was there, Kevin Nugent was on loan from Leyton Orient. You had Phil Harrington who was the goalkeeper… probably, in my estimation, the best goalkeeper Cork City ever had, and he still lives in Cork. His son now is playing in goals for Cork City, and is carrying on the name. You had Gerry McCabe who came in later years.

Some of the pros that came over were terrible altogether. I remember we brought in three Bulgarian internationals, and they just couldn't gel in with us at all. Half of the time they were freezing cold with the Irish weather. They played one or two games and we just never brought them back.

But we had a couple of players that stayed. Mick Conroy stayed and is still living in Cork. Paul Bannon was another great asset to us. Alec Ludzic when he came over… he stayed.

Without doubt, we would be a close group. I could be onto three ex-players in one day... just talking away to them. We always got on. When we played, all of our games were on Sundays. So, when you'd come back from Dublin, you would be out on the Sunday night. There was many a time you wouldn't get home until four or five o'clock on Monday morning... and then go straight to work for 8am.

At that time there were no Friday night games or Saturday night games, because the clubs didn't have lights. Only Dalymount Park and Tolka Park had lights at the time. So, all of our games were on Sunday afternoon.

Training consisted of a warm-up, a bit of stretching first by yourself.

Then we'd have a run. Pre-season running was just unbelievable... you could run about four or five miles no problem before they'd tell you to stop. We'd be out on the pitch and we'd do six laps. He might give us seven and a half minutes to do those six laps of the pitch.

You'd have to do it. When you finished the six laps, you'd have one minute rest. Then you would do five laps in six and a half minutes. Then a one minute rest again... then four laps in five and a half minutes.

It kept on going down, and you'd have a minute of rest. It was always tough, but we used to do it... that would be pre-season. It then made the rest of the season that little bit easier, but you'd still have a good session of running every Tuesday night and you'd be gasping for air halfway through it. We trained one time running up and down the motorcycle track.

When you look at it now, you wouldn't get in there in a million years... how we didn't break an ankle in there as well. Overall, it was different training. I don't know what the players are doing now with regards to training, but I suppose a lot of that would be watching what they eat and maybe doing a bit of weight training, looking at opposition videos and stuff like that.

In our day, we just didn't do any of that. It was just run, run... *run*, and ball work... and more ball work. So, it was just totally different, but it was brilliant at the time for us. We enjoyed it and there was a great bond with the whole lot of us.

You could nearly go back and phone any fella that went through the mill that time. We were all just like one big happy family. It was great.

99

JOHN CAULFIELD

CORK CITY 1 ★ BAYERN MUNICH 1
UEFA Cup First Round First Leg
Musgrave Park
SEPTEMBER 18, 1991

The Cork City team of the early 90s (John Caulfield is second from the right in the front row)
brought such honour to the club, and created history in Europe with some remarkable results
including their performances over two legs against Bayern Munich.

★ **CORK CITY:** P Harrington; L Murphy, D Daly, P Bannon, S Napier, M Conroy, T Kenneally, D Barry, G McCabe, **J Caulfield**, P Morley. Sub: P Coughlan for Conroy.

★ **BAYERN MUNICH:** G Hillringhaus; T Berthold, C Ziege, O Kreuzer, R Grahammer, M Bender, Bernardo, S Effenberg, M Sternkopf, R Wohlfarth, Manzinho. Subs: B Labbadia for Sternkopf, M Schwabl for Bender.

THE ACTION

A PART-TIME SIDE in Cork City against giants of German and European football in Bayern Munich. This on paper appeared to be a real *David* vs *Goliath affair*.

However, if Bayern were expecting an easy workout when they faced City at Musgrave Park, they were given a rude awakening in the 26th minute. Dave Barry scored arguably the most famous goal in Cork City history, when he maintained his composure and controlled well, before finishing well beyond the grasp of visiting netminder Gerald Hillringhaus

Bayern, a side which was full of German internationals, equalised before the half-time whistle. After a shot on goal was initially blocked, the ball broke to Stefan Effenberg and he steered his shot into the bottom corner of the net.

While the game was now being played on Bayern's terms, the Leesiders were by no means forced to withstand an onslaught in the second-half. City had chances through Anthony Kenneally and Pat Morley, but the best opportunity fell to Dave Barry from a free kick, which forced a fine save from Hillringhaus.

While for Bayern, Roland Wohlfarth, who was the previous season's top scorer in the Bundesliga, struck the crossbar, with Manfred Schwabl seeing his strike hit the post.

Bayern would end up seeing the tie out by winning 2-0 in the second leg in Munich, but Cork City had more than held their own in that famous first leg.

★★★★★

66

FOR GENERATIONS AFTERWARDS, looking back, it is hard for them to imagine how we could have played a club that big and got a 1-1 draw in Musgrave Park… against one of the biggest teams in the world.

It was a *Roy of the Rovers* story… how do you tell people nowadays, or those who started following the club in the mid-2000s or whatever, that you drew 1-1 with Bayern Munich, who they see winning the German league and playing in Champions League finals?

At that time, they had so many German internationals… and a Brazilian international. They had already won three or four European Cups. Sometimes I think when you tell people the stories, they even find it hard to believe you. But that is the way it was at the time and it was such a unique occasion. That is why it is such a fantastic memory in Cork City history.

Who do you compare Bayern Munich to? Do you compare them with Juventus, AC Milan, Real Madrid, Barcelona, Liverpool, Man United? So, when you think of it that way, it must be considered one of the greatest results. I know League of Ireland clubs have had good results against Celtic and Rangers. But I think Bayern Munich are a totally different level

There used to be a programme on BBC on a Wednesday night called *Sportsnight*. Basically, it was like *Match of The Day*, but they used to cover all the midweek and European soccer. On the show that night they ended up showing the goal we scored against Bayern Munich and the celebrations afterwards. They said it was probably the greatest result of the day.

When you think of it, the BBC in England finishing up with a League of Ireland club on the programme… I think it showed what type of reaction it created across Europe on that particular day. Absolutely, they would have expected an easier match and, to be fair, in the bigger scheme of things, they are one of the top 10 biggest clubs in the world.

I'd say Noel O'Mahony didn't sleep for a week before the match… knowing Noel. He'd have been fearful that we'd have taken a battering. But still, he would have been excited by how big the draw was.

Noel played with Cork clubs all of his life and he was a real passionate Cork soccer person. Knowing Noel, he'd have been biting his nails and going to church praying. But in fairness to him, he was always very good to make sure we kept our shape. He liked us to be aggressive, and he liked us to be very fit. But at the same time, he recognised we had a lot of very good players, as well. There wouldn't have been video analysis and stuff like that... it hadn't been part of the game as much and certainly not in the League of Ireland.

Certainly, there was not lots of work done on shape; it wouldn't have been to the same level things are done nowadays, which is understandable. At the same time, we had a lot of intelligent players. They knew what to do and their knowledge of the game and how to defend was very good.

Coaching at that time was in some ways better than nowadays, because it was more simplistic. Noel was very good at getting teams set up and organised from that point of view.

We all know how huge German football is. So, I think they thought it was going to be a stroll in the park. I am not sure Bayern Munich would have been very impressed with the surroundings in Musgrave Park either, at the time.

The dressing-rooms were small, and the pitch would have been a bit bumpy. It would not have been the ideal surface for them. But there is no doubt that for us... we wanted to go out and give it our best. You couldn't imagine, however, that you were going to get a draw in the match,

We were looking at keeping it tight, trying to prevent them from scoring goals and trying to keep the score down. But at the same time, we were certainly very fit players. There was a great camaraderie within the group. Throughout the league we had built a very tough and physical team. We still had some tremendous players as well.

We were on the ball very little, because generally they were controlling the game. We were pressing, harassing and tackling... trying to disrupt them, but the funny thing on the day was that we settled into the game very quickly. Bayern were playing their passing game and tried to control the game.

They found that our intensity and pressing quite difficult. Even before we scored, we had been threatening with opportunities. Sometimes in these games, you never get a chance, but you could see early in the match that they were a bit open and that if we could intercept the ball or put them under a bit of pressure... if they made some mistake, then we might get a chance.

We scored and then Effenberg scored before half-time, and certainly in the second-half it was very hard to maintain the intensity that we had. We probably ended up defending a little bit deeper, but there were still occasions in the second-half where had had a couple of half-chances.

Look, there is no doubt we rode our luck and they had chances to win the game. But you need those days when 'Biscuits' (Phil Harrington) was phenomenal in goal, and our defence was fantastic.

It was as if we were sitting in the long grass waiting to pounce on them. I think Mick Conroy won the ball... Pat played a pass across to Dave. The good thing for us that day is that it fell to Dave, because everyone knew and certainly within our team, Dave had the best strike of a ball. From 20, 25 yards he was a brilliant striker of a ball.

When it fell to him, he struck it brilliantly. It might have taken a slight deflection, but it fell to the right man at the right time. It certainly is a huge and iconic goal in the history of Cork City Football Club.

Overall, it was so satisfying to get that result and particularly by the fact that we did have a number of half-chances during the game. It wasn't a game where we just scored one and didn't cross the halfway line for the rest of the game... it wasn't that type of game. As a group we defended really well and I think it probably showed the type of spirit that was in the group and the team at the time.

For a number of years that Cork City team had been challenging at the top, and afterwards won the league. I think it showed we had a very strong built team, a very committed and passionate team. I think that day against Bayern Munich showed a lot of those characteristics.

There is no doubt that Bayern Munich got a massive shock and there is certainly no way they would have expected that the game was going to end 1-1... our enthusiasm and our intensity playing that day certainly upset them.

I think when you look at who Bayern Munich were and the status of the club... they are the biggest club Cork City has ever played in Europe. That is why I always say that result is the greatest for the club in Europe, despite the fact that there were many other great results in Europe by other Cork City teams. It was just the fact that they were such a big football club... and, it may be hard for younger people to understand, but we were a part-time team.

On the morning of the Bayern Munich match we were all working. It was no different to any league match… we were all working that morning, and we met in Musgrave Park.

At that time, of course, the open draw was in; there was no such thing as seeding. So, a small club like us could have drawn anyone. Unfortunately, that changed within a couple of years when the seeding came in.

We got Bayern Munich and everyone remembers what happened… Dave scoring, Effenberg equalising… a real backs-to-the-wall second-half… Phil Harrington made incredible saves… Declan Daly made an unbelievable block on the line. At the end of the day, we rode our luck and gave as good as we got.

That was one of the first breakthroughs for the club at the time. It was a great occasion; there was no stands, but clay banks all around the ground with a crowd of around 5,500. I can think of lots of different moments throughout my career. But when you break through and you start winning trophies at the club… they are always special occasions. European games were obviously special.

We had a very good evening afterwards, but we were all back into training the following night preparing for our league match the following Sunday. That was the way the times were, you just worked in the morning, turned up for the game and then back into work on the Thursday.

The away leg certainly was one of the fantastic moments of our careers because, at that time, Munich were playing in the Olympic Stadium. There was the running track around it, a real open plan stadium… the capacity was about 80,000. The dressing-rooms were incredible and they were absolutely enormous. I think it was a situation where we were going over with no expectations.

The talk around the place was that they were going to hammer us over there. The interesting thing was, we were really looking forward to the game. To our advantage, the beer festival was on at the time over in Munich. We had played Sligo on the Saturday evening. When you look at now and preparation for Europe, every team gets their game cancelled.

But, we were rushing back out of Sligo after losing 2-1, to get the eight o'clock flight out of Cork to Munich on Sunday morning. We were all really bursting with enthusiasm. I don't want to say we didn't care about the Sligo result, but we all wanted to make sure we were ready for Munich.

We arrived in Munich and, as I say, the beer festival was on. The hospitality of Bayern Munich… they brought us out on the Sunday evening to one of the massive marquees in Munich, to sample the beer festival. There was no better group of lads that could enjoy themselves going into an environment like that.

We all went back on the bus to the hotel singing and had a great laugh. We got up on Monday morning to prepare for the match. Noel O'Mahony, decided to run us on the Monday morning… ran us into the ground, and he knocked all the liquid out of us.

The game itself was fantastic because the crowd was around 15,000. The occasion… the pitch was incredibly big and the surface was immaculate. And they were watering the pitch, stuff we had never seen before.

We came in at half-time and it was 0-0.

We actually defended with much ease compared to the game in Cork when they put us under a lot more pressure. But over in Munich, they just found it very difficult to break us down. At half-time all of a sudden, we're thinking… *they haven't put us away and the game is still there.*

One potential goal could have put us through, even though never in your wildest dreams did we think we'd be in that position. As the video of the match shows afterwards, on 70 minutes we had a half-chance in the box. We had a period of four or five minutes when we had a little bit of play that created the chance.

On 75 minutes, they broke away from an attack where we had lost the ball. Three passes later… the ball is in the back of the net. Bayern got the second goal in the 90th minute. Over there in Munich, our performance was probably better than our home performance.

There is no doubt over the two ties they were the better team. But certainly, in the game in Germany they became very edgy and, on another day, maybe we might have scored. One of their big supporters at the time, Boris Becker, he was in the stand. I am not sure what he made of it, but the Bayern players took a lot of stick after the game and there was a lot of criticism that a team like Cork City had run them so close.

DAVE BARRY
(& DECLAN DALY)

SHELBOURNE 2 ★ CORK CITY 3
League Of Ireland Premier Division
Championship Play-Off
RDS Arena
MAY 22, 1993

Dave Barry celebrates in the RDS, after Cork City had clinched the 1993 league title.

★ **SHELBOURNE:** J Byrne; P Coyle, M Neville, A Whelan, K Brady, M Rutherford, G Costelloe, P Doolin, B Browne, G Haylock, P Dully: Sub: B Flood for Dully.

★ **CORK CITY:** P Harrington; C Cotter, D Daly, F O'Donoghue, S Napier, A Buckley, **D Barry**, G McCabe, J Glynn, P Morley, P Bannon. Sub: J Caulfield for Glynn.

THE ACTION

A THRILLING VICTORY over Shelbourne at the RDS helped to secure the league title for Cork City.

It was the first occasion that City secured the Premier Division crown, which arrived after a three-way tie with Shelbourne and Bohemians, and an extended play-off series to decide the championship. A 3-2 win over Shelbourne at the RDS in the sixth play-off game finally earned the club its day of glory.

City took the lead in the 23rd minute. Pat Morley headed into the back of the net, following a clever assist by Anthony Buckley to knee the ball across the goalmouth and into his path.

Gary Haylock, however, slotted home from the penalty spot to get Shels back on level terms prior to half time.

After Shels were reduced to 10 men, City went back in front though a neat finish by Dave Barry. But Shelbourne levelled the game up again when Anto Whelan hammered the ball through a ruck of players before finding the net.

City showed their fighting qualities to bounce back and they got what turned out to be the match-winner in the 74th minute through Paul Bannon.

Gerry McCabe's well executed cross reached Bannon at the far post, and he duly applied the necessary finish.

★★★★★

66

GOING BACK TO 1984, when Cork City was founded, I was asked to join the club. I was playing with the Cork senior gaelic footballers at the time, and I always wanted to try League of Ireland, the top level in this country.

There were no clubs before that for a few years in Cork, after Cork United disbanded.

So, I jumped on board. We brought in a lot of young fellas from England at this stage, such as Dave Bleasdale and Bobby Woodruff, good young fellas, but they were probably 19 or 20 at the time.

In those first years it was extremely difficult because they didn't really work out. We were playing out in Flower Lodge, and it was hard to get the crowds in.

But I have to say, going through all of those early years, just keeping the club in the Premier Division was extremely difficult. Just not getting relegated and staying in the top division was a big achievement at the time because there wasn't a lot of money around Cork at that stage. It was just about staying afloat, really.

The 'one game' for me, definitely, would be at the RDS when we won the league… with a lot of lads that I played with, we were striving there for many, *many* years. I remember we got to the FAI Cup final in 1989 and even that year we were down battling relegation… third or fourth from the bottom of the league.

For us to lose it in Turner's Cross on the last day of the season in 1991 against Dundalk, when Tom McNulty got the winner for them and they went on to win the league… it was extremely disappointing. To go up to the RDS and win the league then, was fantastic for us really.

People knew I was playing with the Cork senior footballers.

In the late 80s people were wondering why I was still playing with Cork City. I was having so much success with the Cork footballers. But Cork City is my home club. I had a couple of opportunities to leave and sign with other clubs, but it was never in my thoughts. I played GAA with Cork and you can't go to another county.

That was the way I looked at it with Cork City as well. If I was going to achieve anything in soccer, I wanted to do it with Cork City… win a league with Cork City, and win cups with Cork City.

That was my ambition, and even though the money wasn't in the club for many of the years that I played there, there still was a great passion and great people running the club. So, to achieve that dream was tremendous really in the RDS.

A lot of people would know the story that after the whole season finished, there were three clubs involved who had a chance of winning it, and we went into a round-robin play-off. We all went down to Kinsale, where we listened to the last game of the season. Whoever won that game would have won the league. It turned out that the two teams involved drew it.

It meant ourselves, Shels and Bohs went into the round-robin and we had a chance to go on and win it. We played one game in Turner's Cross… Pat Morley scored down there. But it finally came down to a decisive game between ourselves and Shels.

A massive, *massive* support we got from the Cork public. The City fans travelled in their thousands up to the RDS. When I look at careers, I think a lot of players spend most of their career winning nothing, just fighting to do well or fighting relegation.

Every team we came up against had outstanding players. To go into the heart of Dublin, and to go to the RDS, after losing in Turner's Cross to win the league of the last day of the season…there was no way we were coming out of the RDS without winning. It was a cracking game and the goals were flying in.

I was lucky enough to score one of them. Paul Bannon, God rest his soul, clinched it for us and we got out of there after winning 3-2. For all of the disappointments I had with Cork City and things like that, it was absolutely a joyous moment.

Noel O'Mahony was a tremendous stalwart for the League of Ireland in Cork. He kept everything going. He was a great personal friend of my uncle as well, so they were up in my house a lot of the time when I was 17 or 18, trying to get me playing League of Ireland.

With Noel managing us as well, it made it that more special.

For me, it was never about money. I never played sport for money. People would have said he'll play with Cork City if there was a clash with the GAA and he must be getting a back-hander. There was no back-hander. There were no big pay-outs. It was just what I grew up with… I grew up in Clareville, a 10-minute walk from Turner's Cross.

We used to go up to Flower Lodge and watch Cork Hibs and Cork Celtic with my dad. I grew up enjoying soccer and GAA. So, it was in my blood and you just played for the love of the game and the love of the club. It came down to that, really.

Everybody knew I was a dual player. I got into a lot of trouble from the Cork County Board because I played with Cork City. They wanted to stop me in 1987 and they asked me to pack up Cork City... or else I wouldn't get onto the Cork team. They gave me an ultimatum, and the worst thing you can give me is that. I am very loyal to whoever I play for. Put a gun to my head and say you have to give up soccer? It was never going to happen. So, I missed out on the 1987 All-Ireland football final.

But they asked me back! Billy Morgan was a great friend of mine, and Billy got me back in '88. I was lucky enough to go on and win two All-Irelands in those years.

After achieving that and doing 'the double' in 1990, which was phenomenal really for the Cork hurlers and footballers, it was always my dream to do more and try to do more with Cork City. I put all of my energy into trying to win a league. To actually achieve that in 1993 against Shelbourne was fantastic, a dream come true really for me on a personal level.

If I look at that team that went into the RDS, and compare it to what Dundalk and Shamrock Rovers could do with their money... they could bring in the best players.

Mick Conroy didn't play in the RDS. Mick was assistant manager to Noel O'Mahony, and Mick had a connection with Gerry McCabe. Gerry came over and was an outstanding player for us. But Mick Conroy coming to us, after playing with Celtic and winning league titles in Scotland, that was a huge boost to us. Paul Bannon used to keep reminding us Mick played against Maradona.

Having these boys around... like Phil Harrington. Phil, for me, was probably the best goalkeeper there at the time. You need these players in there and you have to have players with that experience. We tried it with the amateur scene around Cork, bringing players up from the Munster Senior League.

I played Munster Senior League and a lot of us came through that league, but you need those three or four fellas on the pitch who can bring that experience to the set up. I think Bannon, Conroy and Phil Harrington... Gerry McCabe, they brought that to us.

In Turner's Cross in 1991, when we lost the league, we only needed a point and we left it after us. In 1992 as well, against Bohs in Lansdowne Road, we left it behind us too... a Dave Tilson goal beat us that day.

I definitely knew going up to Dublin there was no way we were coming out of there without the trophy. I personally tried to bring that into management as well. When I took over, it was as a semi-pro, but when we went out onto the pitch it was about winning games. It wasn't about anything else... we went out to win.

A lot of the times we didn't win, but with that mentality that was in the dressing-room that year, definitely up in the RDS there was no way were coming back on the bus or train coming home to Cork without the trophy. This was our chance and we weren't leaving it behind. We went ahead, got pegged back... sucker-blows to us, really. But nobody dropped their heads.

It was right until the end! We scored late in the game, that winner through Paul Bannon. But that was because we were all experienced at that stage and were after going through a lot. I think that stood to us late in the game.

I think Noel O'Mahony, to be fair to him, was always battling. He was taking over teams in Cork at a time when there was no money. Every team he had wasn't financed, really... they were always living on scraps.

But Noel brought a real competitiveness into the dressing-room. We were always competitive with Noel. Even in a Munster Cup game against a Munster Senior League side, we'd always go out and he'd always want to win.

Then when we went abroad, if anybody didn't give one hundred percent Noel would be down on your back. It was more a fighting spirit that Noel brought to us, a never say die attitude... no matter who we were up against. He built a mentality that we are going to make it hard for whoever we are playing.

That goes for all of the European games we played, as well. That is what we had... that and a great camaraderie in the dressing-room. I feel sorry for young fellas now because with social media, they can't go out for a pint.

But we used to have a bonding session every weekend. That team... we all went to each other's weddings, and we drank together at the weekends. We celebrated... and when we got beaten, we downed our sorrows together too. That is how tight knit that group was.

It was more or less the same squad all of those years. Though, the special players were still so important, as I've said, like Mick Conroy. Pat Morley was probably the best striker in the League of Ireland for probably five or six years. For my goal against Bayern Munich, that people talk about, Morley got the ball and gave it to me. But Mick Conroy's tackle made that goal…and Morley, it was his first touch that put me through. That whole moment and the goal was down to the experience and instinct of really good, experienced players like Pat and Mick.

Every time I went back playing with Cork City, people would have a slag at me… telling me they are no good, they'll never win anything… they will never do anything!

I had listened to that since I came into the League of Ireland. To actually rock the boat, to actually take over as a manager then and to get players who I felt were able to compete at League of Ireland level and to go on and bring home one of the iconic cups, that was so satisfying. As a player, I had helped bring back Cork City's first league title. Then to bring back the FAI Cup for the first time to the club, that was very special too. Especially with my background… my grandfather and great grandfather had won the FAI Cup as players.

I lost two cup finals, so to actually do it as a manager was a tremendous feeling, really.

It comes down to enjoyment, it comes down to playing for your own club and your own city. As I said, other clubs around the league were wondering… would I ever leave? I used to travel around Europe with the League of Ireland side, and I'd sit down and talk to other players and they wanted to know would I ever leave Cork City and go to any other club?

They'd find out that Cork was my club.

I loved playing in Cork and if I wanted to win anything, I wanted to win it with my club and my people. That is what it boils down to. It is a passion. At this stage now it has gone professional in the league and I wouldn't blame anybody leaving clubs and trying to make a career of it… make some money and pay the mortgage. It is a different scenario now. Whereas, I was working and only played semi-professional.

As I've said, it didn't come down to money for a lot of us. If you look at the squads that we had, a lot of lads would have played seven, eight, nine… 10 years with Cork City. It was a love and passion, and a great environment to play football.

For me, that is what it boiled down to.

99

DECLAN DALY

Declan Daly enjoys the company of Republic of Ireland manager Jack Charlton after raising the League of Ireland trophy as Cork City skipper in 1993.

66

WE HAD LOST the league decider a couple of years earlier to Dundalk in Turner's Cross. That was a sore defeat because we had done so well during that season. To lose at the last minute, it was a big blow for us.

We had a really good side at the time. It was the longest league season probably in 1993 because of the way it was designed, but the reason the win stands out for me is because it was a counterbalance to the Dundalk defeat.

I don't think I ever felt so low after a game than I did after Dundalk. So, to have that feeling of elation after the Shels match… it was amazing.

I think the whole experience of that season was a bit of a rollercoaster ride.

It was a really strange season in that it went into a play-off to decide the title, and then it came down to the last game against Shels in the RDS, which we won after a thriller. All of that combined is why 'that game' was the key one for me.

A lot of the Shels players, like Paul Doolin and Mick Neville, had won numerous leagues. They were all top-class players, and we always had good battles with them, but I'd like to think we broke even with them mostly. On the day it mattered in the RDS, we actually came out on top.

The long season ended with a play-off…. with three teams tied up. It was down to a round-robin series of games between us, Bohs and Shels to decide the title.

It was ironic that we were defeated by Dundalk by a Tom McNulty goal in Turner's Cross, because in 1993, McNulty scored against Bohs in Oriel Park to actually bring around the play-off.

It was a unique season, and a season where there was no goal difference that was going to decide the league. Going into the last game of the season, there were three teams who could have potentially won the title, depending on results.

One of the games was Bohs and Dundalk, and their game was delayed because Bohs got caught up in traffic on the way to Dundalk. We were actually in Bishopstown, and our game was finished… and we were waiting on the result from Bohs, because Bohs could have effectively won the league that day.

The day itself, when we clinched the title in the RDS, was brilliant. We went up, and a huge crowd from Cork travelled as usual. Shelbourne were a really strong side at the time. It was 3-2 in the end… but there was so much ebbing and flowing as it went along. There were goals, and there were chances created.

At the end, to get the trophy into our hands, the first time Cork City had won the league… it was a huge, *huge* relief.

There was the whole sense of anticipation, and the atmosphere in the dressing-room beforehand. Then going onto the pitch… the highs, and then the lows when you conceded a goal, and to go back and score again.

There is no overriding incident from the game that sticks out for me, only the whole tension that went with the game right through.

In the dressing-room beforehand, there was a huge belief that we were going to win the game and that we are going to take the title back home with us. Then afterwards, in the same room, just sitting with the trophy… looking at it, and soaking it all in. That memory at the end is the strongest memory that I have from it.

I think as well, even the players we had who came in from outside of Cork…

they all lived in Cork, and they all understood what it meant to play sport in Cork. They all understood what it meant to try and win for a team in Cork. They were embedded in the city, and they were as Cork as we were.

They all wanted to do it for the city as much as we did.

Even to this day, a lot of them are still here. Phil Harrington is a prime example... he is still here in Cork. They all loved the club and they all wanted to win for the club, Really, there was no separation between who was from Cork and who wasn't.

At that stage, everybody was the same.

We all wanted the same thing, which was to win for our club and that was it. There was a belief, but we also had a really good side at the time.

Shelbourne had players who I admired hugely, like Mick Neville and those kind of players who were some of the better players that I have played against. They had a scattering of those star players in their team, and they were really strong. But going up to play Shelbourne, I didn't have any fear going into that game in the RDS.

Noel O'Mahony had this enormous knowledge of League of Ireland.

He loved the League of Ireland. He brought his passion to the whole equation. He wore that passion on his sleeve, and it was infectious in the dressing-room. Noel brought the whole package to the dressing-room, which was really important. That passion and that Corkness... that desire to win, and repeat what he had done himself as a player. Equally, Jerry Harris... he was an ever present at any of the games that I was involved in with Cork City.

I can remember when the whistle went.

You are just numb and don't know what has happened... you just know it's finished. Then the realisation hits, when the fans are on the pitch and there is happiness everywhere around you! Obviously, there is desolation on the side of Shels, but we had been there before as well.

The realisation that the whistle had gone... *we had won*. We were getting the trophy.

Then, when the presentation stand is set up and they are actually going to give you the trophy, that is when the penny drops... and you finally soak it all in.

I have often said this, but the beauty about living in Cork is that it is a sports mad place. Invariably, the supporters in Cork... support Cork. Whatever your sport really, they will always support and always want Cork to do well.

Whether it is basketball, hurling, gaelic football, soccer, rugby, camogie, ladies football... whatever it is, once you are from Cork everybody wants you to do well. That is the way it is. The people are passionate about it and the expectation is that you are going to win things. With that comes a lot of pressure. But that is the beauty of playing here and that is why it was great to play with Cork City FC.

It was huge. On that day I was lucky enough to be captain of the side. But anybody could have been captain of that Cork City team because they were a good side. I was just the one that was lucky enough to be picked to collect the silverware.

It is fabulous and as I say, Cork is so sports mad that if you can achieve something like we did at that time, and subsequently the FAI Cup win and the League Cup... whatever victories you have at Cork City are hugely appreciated by the people.

When we came back with that league trophy the following day and the following night, we went over to what at that time was Guinness House. We were over there, and there was a crowd outside waiting to see the trophy and to welcome us home. The whole occasion was just huge.

During my time playing, we went from an era of part-time football to an era of full-time football. At that time most of the team probably trained twice or three times a week, then we played at the weekends. Sometimes it started on a Sunday. Then Friday fixtures came in.

The average age of our team when we won the league would have been high twenties, maybe even thirties. Whereas now, the League of Ireland seems to be made up of far younger players.

I had 18 or 19 years playing, between Limerick and Cork City, but mostly with Cork and I had nothing but good times.

I know we had defeats with Cork City that were very hard to take... the cup final against Bohs... the league decider against Dundalk in Turner's Cross.

We lost other leagues that we felt we should have won perhaps too. But we had such highlights, like that day in the RDS, and also the European games. In those European games we were pitting ourselves against, at that time because it was an open draw, the best in Europe.

We got Bayern Munich, Galatasaray, Slavia Prague... all of those teams. To play against those teams, and the level that they were playing at, was always a huge highlight.

I had an exceptionally lucky career. I loved every bit of it. It has had a huge impact on my life.

DEREK COUGHLAN
(& PATSY FREYNE)

CORK CITY 1 ★ SHELBOURNE 0
FAI Cup Final Replay
Dalymount Park
MAY 16, 1998

Derek Coughlan celebrates a goal at Turner's Cross with teammate John O'Flynn in 2005, after his return to Cork City.

★ **CORK CITY:** N Mooney; F O'Donoghue, **D Coughlan**, D Daly, G Cronin, K Flanagan, P Freyne, D Hill, O Cahill, J Caulfield, N Hartigan. Subs: J Glynn for Hartigan, P Long for O'Donoghue.

★ **SHELBOURNE:** A Gough; D Smith, P Scully, T McCarthy, D Geoghegan, L Kelly, D Fitzgerald, P Fenlon, M Rutherford, S Geoghegan, D Baker. Subs: M Neville for Fitzgerald, P Morley and T Sheridan for Geoghegan and Rutherford.

THE ACTION

DEREK COUGHLAN WAS the hero when Cork City secured FAI Cup glory as they defeated Shelbourne in this final replay at Dalymount Park.

It was the first occasion that the FAI Cup was heading back to Leeside in 25 years.

The victory also was a landmark occasion for City manager and former player Dave Barry, with the Cork GAA star assembling a playing group at City with a good mix of youth and experience.

City goalkeeper Noel Mooney was forced into making a fine save on 31 minutes to keep out a screamer from Pat Fenlon. But Cork upped the ante in the second-half and Gareth Cronin forced Shels' goalkeeper Alan Gough into action.

With Patsy Freyne and Dave Hill starting to take control in the middle of the park, the Leesiders were seeing the better of the exchanges.

Then City struck with the decisive blow. From a Kelvin Flanagan corner kick, Coughlan rose the highest inside the penalty area to direct his header into the corner of the net.

★★★★★

66

SCORING THE ONLY goal in a replay, and Cork winning the cup for the first time in 25 years, it was a game that defines my career.

Not many players get to experience playing in an FAI Cup final, never mind winning it. I was fortunate enough to score, and that goal was a great catalyst in my career.

Pat Scully was marking me for set-pieces as Kelvin Flanagan put in a corner in the 73rd minute of the game. I peeled to the back post, and got my head to it. I will never forget just having that rush of adrenaline after scoring. I went jumping on the fence where all the Cork City fans were in Dalymount Park, with Johnny Glynn on my back.

When the celebrations stopped and I was running back down the pitch, I actually felt drained from the rush of adrenaline I had just experienced.

I will never forget thinking… *we have got to make sure that they don't score now… make sure that this wins us the cup.* That was the task, and it was a long 20 minutes trying to keep Shels from scoring

Growing up, you are pretending to be in cup finals, reading the *Roy Of The Rovers* annuals… and getting that goal had a feeling of that about it. All the practice paid off when I got my head on Kelvin's cross. It was a dream come true to win that silverware for Cork City.

When the final whistle blew and the celebrations began, it was a fantastic feeling to have played a role in securing that win. Shels were a phenomenal team, with the likes of Pat Morley, Pat Scully, the Geoghegans… and Tony Sheridan and Pat Fenlon. When you look at the line-ups of the two teams, it was a huge clash.

To beat Shels and to win that game against them up in Dublin in a replay, keeping a clean sheet in both games, it was really special.

When we eventually went up the steps to lift the cup, I looked over and saw my parents. My dad had tears rolling down his face. This was a man who won an All-Ireland football medal in 1973.

That is my one outstanding memory of the day. It was a memorable moment after all the support they had given me throughout the years of ups and downs.

Only recently, a fella came up to me and said he had 20 quid on me to get the first goal. So, he made a few bob out of it. A lot of the younger lads don't know about it, but some of the older generations bring it up with me and I love talking about it. It is something I am very proud of... something that will live with me forever.

The crowd were unbelievable.

There was a big attendance for the first game in Dalymount Park and a lot of them came back up for the replay six days later. I went close with a header in the first match, that went just over the bar. I remember all week feeling that I was going to score and that visualisation only got stronger as we approached the ground on the bus.

I was listening to my pre-match music on my Discman, looking out the window, and it gave me goosebumps seeing all the fans welcoming us to the old stadium.

The Cork City fans chanting and cheering got louder the closer we got to Dalymount, it felt like we were going into battle. Lifting the cup sparked massive celebrations.

I do remember that we had quite a bit of luck and it felt like our name was on the cup. Things went right! Derry got an outrageous OG in one of the rounds. We got Athlone in the semi-final, and Jason Kabia got a couple of goals that day... I think we won 3-1. I just felt that there was something special in the squad and a sense that we were going to win something that year. In the FAI Cup, then, things just started to go our way.

Winning the cup with the likes of Decky Daly, John Caulfield, Fergie O'Donoghue, Philip Long and Patsy Freyne... all of these iconic Cork players. You had young players like Colin O'Brien, Ollie Cahill and Brian Barry-Murphy in the team as well.

We were part-time, but we were up against that very good St Pat's team that pipped us and we were runners-up in the Premier Division. We came very close a couple of times. We won the League Cup that same year. It would have been a shame if that group of players under Dave Barry never came away with silverware.

Luckily enough, we did it that year.

The team was full of fantastic players with different traits. Two players that stood out for me were Patsy Freyne and Ollie Cahill... unbelievable street footballers, they loved taking players on.

I am still great friends with all of the lads. I made friends for life. We always had each other's back on the pitch and when we meet each other now, there's a bond between us. You just had some brilliant characters in the squad, and I'm thankful to have experienced winning the cup with that group.

It was a massive learning point when I came back from England and Brighton in 1996. I was in with proper men and winners, fellas with high standards. It took me a year or so to start getting to the pitch of where I needed to be, to mix it with these lads and to be a part of them. So to be around the likes of Declan Daly, John Caulfield and Dave Hill, Philip Long... and when I came home first, Dave Barry was still actually playing as well. I think just being around those players was a massive help for me. It helped me set the standards that I needed to have for a successful career ahead of me.

It was definitely the best thing that I ever did. For the two years I spent over there in England, I was homesick every week. There was no question after the two years were up that I wasn't coming home. I couldn't book my ticket home fast enough.

When I came back, I remember meeting Dave Barry in the sitting room with my mam and dad. It really kick-started my career. I think there is a bit of a difference between the dressing-rooms in Ireland and England, back then especially.

Just the type of characters, and these lads had to have a career outside of football as well. They had great values. It was a more mature environment coming back and being part of a League of Ireland dressing-room.

Training facilities were rough and ready. It was whatever we could find, and whatever place we could train on. At times that year, we were training in Ballinhassig. It was a muddy field covered in hoof marks and, one night, we had the car lights on to illuminate the pitch.

Everyone was working, so we'd train in the evening time. We trained Tuesday, Thursday and Saturday morning, before playing a match then on a Sunday at two o'clock. There were times we used to train out on the Lough when we wouldn't have a pitch and we'd play out there in between the trees. You faced the risk of going over on your ankle from the roots of the trees.

It was whatever you needed to do to be successful. You just had to roll your sleeves up and do it. There was no point complaining or wishing for anything different. It was what it was. The alternative was to whinge and moan… or you could roll your sleeves up to try and make the team successful and bring success to Cork. That was the benefit of having those strong characters in the dressing-room. I think they steered the ship and made sure that all of us young lads had the same values and standards. With Dave Barry, there was no room for anyone not pulling their weight. Every practice game was full blooded, like it was a cup final.

I had a big GAA background. My dad played GAA and I played GAA up to Cork minor. So, Dave Barry would have been a hero and I would have had his autograph, especially from the GAA side of things, but also from the soccer. He was a Cork stalwart to me and, to be honest, I don't think he gets the credit he deserves. To be such a success in two totally different sports, it is unheard of! It is very hard to think of people who have got to the levels Dave Barry got to in the two most participated sports in this country.

When I came back from Brighton, Dave wasn't long arriving to my house to sign me. The minute he came and said that he wanted me to play for Cork City, I was just looking for the pen because he was such a hero of mine.

I was Cork through and through. I just loved playing for my city and my county. Wearing that Cork City jersey was something that meant an awful lot to me. When I met the then manager Liam Murphy, after the 2001 season, I realised that I wasn't part of his plans. I wasn't sure what I was going to do, until Stephen Kenny rang me and I was delighted to sign for Bohemians and we went on to win the league with a phenomenal team including Kevin Hunt, Glen Crowe, Mark Rutherford and Colin Hawkins.

I came back to Cork City and finished off in style by winning the league in 2005 with another fantastic team. I retired after the FAI Cup final loss that year when I was 28 years of age.

The 1998 FAI Cup win spring-boarded my career… scoring that goal gave me more belief and it gave me momentum. I went on to score quite a few goals after that. So, the cup final goal gave me the boost of confidence which every player needs, that reassurance that you are able to play at the highest level in the country.

That goal did that for me, and it opened a lot of doors for me afterwards as well. Being able to win the cup after it being gone from Cork since 1973, with all of those special players that I have mentioned. It did shape thing. I love the fact that it is part of my journey. It is something that I am extremely proud of!

My big memory is my dad's face as I collected the medal. I looked over and he was only about 20 or 30 feet away. Seeing his fist up and the tears going down his face… my dad was my hero and my best friend. He is gone almost 10 years now. So, that memory of how much it meant to him, that is when I realised how big a deal it was. I think the emotion got to him after all the years of being dragged from the comfort of his armchair into all kinds of weather, to come out with me on the street and practice pretend cup final-winning goals.

PATSY FREYNE

Patsy Freyne in action against Derry City in Turner's Cross in 2000.

66

I NEVER WON a league title, so the one game that sticks out from my career is winning the FAI Cup in 1998. I was 34 when we did it, so it kind of proved to myself that I was half-decent… and that I could win something!

I don't think I was ever in the game for personal achievements. When you are playing for your own team and your own club, all we ever wanted to do was for Cork City to do well.

Winning it was brilliant. It was great for the club and great for the town. When Davy Barry asked me to come back, I just wanted to go again and see that the club could compete. I would never say I won this cup… I would say we won the cup. It wasn't an individual thing with me at all.

That is just the way it is. I was never fortunate enough to win the league, as I say, but that's the way it goes. The FAI Cup we won in 1998 under Dave… there were a few of the older boys still around, like myself, Caulfield, Decky… Biscuits. Then Dave brought in a couple of very young lads as well, the likes of Ollie Cahill and Derek Coughlan.

It was exciting times. Davy turned it around with the help of the board. The run to the final itself was brilliant. When you go all the way and look back on games, they were very tight. In the second round we won by an own goal, 1-0. But you need to have luck when you win anything.

It is not that we were lucky to win the game, but the goal was lucky.

The semi-final above in Athlone… we won 3-1. But the atmosphere from the Cork City supporters, I will never ever forget. It was an unbelievable atmosphere, and obviously the win made it better again. The first game of the final was drawn and it was a hard contest… you had to work hard. In the replay, we won with Derek Coughlan's goal.

I was supposed to be packing up after that game. It was supposed to be my last game. So, it just meant everything to me to try and go out with a win. I didn't retire, and Davy changed my mind after.

I actually got Man of the Match, but I didn't give a f**k about myself. It was just the winning of the game that was the thing. I know there is a Man of the Match award, but you don't win anything on your own. It is a team, and I always felt that. It was a real team effort. With the likes of Caulfield, Decky and Biscuits, it was a real team effort and there were none of us won anything on our own.

We were real Cork people trying to win games for Cork City. That's what it felt like to play for the club… it was a privilege. I wish I could still be playing now, but sure that's the way it goes.

Look at the crowds back then… a huge crowd from Cork going up for the final twice, for the first game and the replay. Then you win it and you are looking at the supporters, it doesn't get any better than that.

Just to see the light on people's faces, it was brilliant.

It doesn't get any better than that, it is as simple as that… in a sporting career it just doesn't get any better. Knowing that you worked hard all year and getting something at the end of it. The supporters are paying their money and you win something, and everyone goes home happy. That is what it is all about at the end of the day. There are enough of downs, so it is brilliant to end on a high. You played the game to win. You make a lot of friends along the way, but when you are on the pitch you are not there to make friends at all. All you are out there for is to win. That particular year was like dying and going to heaven. It was a brilliant, *brilliant* year.

I am sure everyone would say the same in any trophy-winning team. There is just a special buzz about the place and a special buzz about the team. I wish I could go out and play again just one more time… going out in Turner's Cross and playing. We were very unlucky not to win the league, that team.

I think what happened, when you look back on it and I've always said it, if the lads I mentioned were a couple of years younger! I think I was 34 when we won the cup. We had come second twice in the league. I always thought if we were a couple of years younger and them lads like Ollie Cahill and Derek Coughlan were a couple of years older… if that team was together in those circumstances, I think we could have probably won a few leagues, but it wasn't to be.

Dave's management… that was the cup that defined him as a manager. I had played with Dave Barry for so long. I wasn't playing and he brought me in. The reason I went back playing, it was because Dave was manager. I don't think I would have gone back for anyone else. With me personally, he just let me play and I was just much freer on the pitch.

He had no airs or graces, and you could talk to him. He was very honest in his approach. He would tell us what he thought and we'd try to go out to do what he said. We had no qualms about it.

We knew him as a player and he was such a great player, that we trusted him in everything that he said. Dave was like us… he just wanted the club to do well. There was no other motive for Dave, he wasn't managing for the money or anything like that. He just wanted Cork City to do well. We were just an extension of that then. As a manager he was brilliant to play under and it just felt comfortable.

Going from being nearly relegated, to nearly winning the league, and winning the FAI cup… and we won a League Cup as well. It was exciting times for the club itself, and the city because the attendances were huge. It was a pleasure and a privilege to play for Cork City at that time because of what it meant to people around, and we were always looking forward to playing in Turner's Cross.

I always enjoyed playing in the cup for some reason.

I just thought it was different to the league, a different atmosphere in games and things like that. There was a great buzz around the place. I always thought playing for Cork City was a privilege in the way that you are playing for your own.

There always has been English players who have come over to help us out. Biscuits was playing… you had Dave Hill at the time as well, and Jason Kabia. The likes of them good lads, they are still around the town. They bought into the club and the city. They are living here now. I was asked to go to Dublin to play and I am sure there were other lads that were asked to go… where you could double or treble your money.

But I don't think that is why we were playing. It definitely wasn't about the money. I know Hilly was probably professional and the English lads, which was fair enough as they were coming from England. For me anyway, it was that I was representing my city and my county, that was the way I felt about it.

Walking out onto Turner's Cross before a game, every single time I felt that I was privileged. I just wanted to play for Cork City and I wanted to do my best for Cork City. That was all that mattered to me. The financial thing, it didn't exist at the time the way it does today. I am not even talking about England, because here in Ireland it is too easy to move.

You get lads going Cork, Dublin, Derry, Galway… because it is a professional game now and they probably have to make as much as they can.

Ollie Cahill went up to Shelbourne. But I never had a problem with that because he was a young lad and it was a no-brainer. But for us and the lads I mentioned a while ago, I don't think it was ever about the money. It was just an honour to play for the club.

For the older lads, we just wanted the club to do well. We'd do through walls for the club at the time. You were playing for your teammates, your manager and your club. Shelbourne were the team that had the money. They bought all the best players in Dublin because they had that money.

They were the team at the time. What Dundalk have done is probably historic, but you are talking about different days then. I would suggest that it was probably easier for Dundalk and Cork City in more recent times because there was only a couple of teams that were professional.

It was more of an even keel long ago, in that everyone was part-time. Even the team that won the league in 2005, there were only a couple of teams professional at that time. And professionals will always beat amateurs, no matter what way you go about it.

We hadn't won the cup for so long.

Cork Hibs were the last team to win it, and that was in 1973. We never won the league, but we had a belief that the team was good enough. I think people, especially the younger lads… it is very important to believe that they can do things. I think that win in 1998 gave fierce confidence to the younger lads, understanding that we are a good side and we can do things here.

Decky Daly was our captain for years and was inspirational to have around. Any problems or anything, you'd go to Decky and he'd sort them out for you. Dave was the manager. But in terms of captains, you'd appoint Decky Daly to be captain all day long. For me, Decky was the captain of the club and I think nobody would begrudge him that. He just had everybody's respect.

For some reason, you always get bigger crowds for the cup games than you would for league games. That is just the way it is in Cork and, I suppose, for most places as well. For myself and the likes of Biscuits, Caulfield, Decky… we had all played with Dave. So, it was easy for us. The younger lads just looked up to him.

He had that awe about him, that whatever he said… they just did it. They didn't question him or anything and I don't think anyone ever questioned what he said. He trusted them and it paid off for him. Ollie Cahill and Derek Coughlan, Noel Hartigan… there were a lot of young lads. They all had fabulous careers after, and it was down to Dave who started them off really.

I always trusted the fellas I played with, but I always put that pressure on myself to play well. Looking across the dressing-room, you had Decky Daly, John Caulfield and Hilly… Phil Harrington wasn't playing at the time, it was Noel Mooney that was in goal.

Then you had all the young lads. Stephen Napier was a brilliant lad… he had played the first game and he was in hospital for the second replay. Fergus O'Donoghue came in and he was outstanding on the night. He had been around early in the club as well and won the league. So, there were obviously winners in the team. But it was definitely more of a collective thing than individual thing. There was good players, but we were better as a team.

I think there was something about playing for Cork City that you just went that extra mile. Especially if you were playing one of the Dublin teams. It was just a brilliant time, a brilliant time for the club. We were doing well and there were great crowds just looking forward to going to Turner's Cross.

I still go to Turner' Cross, because I am just like them supporters at the end of the day, I am just a supporter now. That goes back to what I said from the start, there was a group of us there and all we wanted was for the club to do well. It passed onto the next generation and that is great.

It kind of kills us now. John Caulfield is up in Galway, but I know it kills him to see Cork City down in the First Division. He'd still think that way, even though he is the manager of Galway United. Dave Barry won't like seeing the club the way it is, Decky Daly, Biscuits… all we talk about is the club and how is it getting on.

I just want the club to do well. I think people just remember how honest you were and how passionate you were for the team. That goes a long way.

I think that is why I was probably remembered, and the older boys. I am only guessing, but if you wear your heart on your sleeve and give your best, I think people can see that. We played for a long time and it is brilliant to be remembered and to be associated with the club.

OLLIE CAHILL

CORK CITY 2 ★ CSKA KYIV 1
UEFA Cup Winners Cup
Turner's Cross
AUGUST 13, 1998

Ollie Cahill is tackled by Valentyn Hrehul of CSKA Kyiv during the UEFA Cup Winners Cup
second leg at Dynamo Stadium in Kiev.

★ **CORK CITY:** N Mooney; D Daly, D Coughlan, D Hill, G Cronin, G O'Halloran, K Flanagan, P Freyne, B Barry-Murphy, **O Cahill**, N Hartigan. Subs: J Kabia for Hartigan, M Herrick for Freyne, J Caulfield for O'Halloran.

★ **CSKA KIEV:** V Reva; V Levchenko, S Revut, V Daraselia, D Semchuk, S Bezhenar, O Oliynik, P Shkapenko, S Zakarlyuka, V Leonenko, E Tsikhmeystruk. Subs: O Oleksienko for Zakarlyuka, D Korenev for Tsikhmeystruk, A Karyaka for Leonenko.

THE ACTION

CORK CITY SECURED an impressive European victory by defeating Ukrainian Cup finalists CSKA Kyiv at Turner's Cross in the UEFA Cup Winners Cup qualifying round first leg.

For City, playing their first home game of the campaign, there were many heroes. One of those was City manager Dave Barry, who mapped out a game plan that worked and gained maximum effort from his players.

Barry, who scored that famous goal for City in a European tie against Bayern Munich, could hardly believe his eyes as his team took the lead against CSKA from the penalty spot in the 20th minute, after Brian Barry-Murphy was taken down inside the box by Bezhenar.

Up stepped Kelvin Flanagan to score with a crisply taken spot kick to the corner of the net.

Things got even better for the home side when City extended their advantage before the end of the first-half. Ollie Cahill went on a driving run down the wing before putting a good ball into the box, which was met by the head of Derek Coughlan, powerfully hitting the back of the net.

Deep into stoppage time, CSKA got a crucial away goal when Sergiy Revut fired home with a scrambled effort from a corner kick.

★★★★★

66

THE GAME THAT always comes back to me in my mind is the European game against CSKA Kyiv in Turner's Cross. We beat them 2-1 on the night. They scored, I think, in the 92nd or 93rd minute from a corner but they had barely threatened all night.

We were really, *really* good on the night. It was a lovely evening and there was a big crowd in Turner's Cross. Playing in Europe as well, I always felt an extra buzz and there was an added anticipation. European Football was where you really tested yourself as a League of Ireland player… trying to get in with the big guns.

That is the platform you want to play on and always trying to better yourself. To get in there and play against CSKA Kyiv and perform the way that we did, that is one I keep coming back to and it sticks out in my mind.

It was a pity we didn't go on to win the tie, as we got beaten 2-0 away in the second leg. But that first leg was one of the highlights for me as a one-off game playing for City. When you think of Kyiv, you think of Dynamo Kyiv and the massive pedigree they have.

Against a team coming from Kyiv and playing in Europe, you are thinking *these will be decent.* But we had a belief in ourselves as well and knew what we were about. We had some really good players and a really good squad.

We were well prepared going into the game. We weren't thinking this is what you are going up against here. We thought, if we could play the way we could play, we could cause problems for most teams.

We had a flavour for Europe from the Intertoto Cup.

We had played Cologne in Turner's Cross. They beat us 2-0, but we kind of put it up to them. The likes of Standard Liege as well. So, we knew on our day we'd be able to give anyone a game, especially in Turner's Cross. We were really looking forward to the contest.

Just those European games in general, they are extra special. The coverage and national coverage you get, you can feel it around the city. You could even feel it in the squad and amongst the players… there was an extra pep in our step and that buzz of playing in those European ties… I used to love it

Kelvin Flanagan scored a penalty. I knocked the ball to Brian Barry-Murphy, and he got taken down and Kelvin tucked it away to put us 1-0 up. We were going well. It was still in the first-half, and I actually got the ball on the wing. I managed to get around one or two players, looked up and Derek Coughlan was in the box. I managed to dink it up and picked him out at the back post and he buried the header.

As a winger, that is your job as such, to be creating for others. So that was just sweet the way it came about, and I was able to get past a couple of players, then pick out that pinpoint cross for Derek to stick it home to put us 2-0 up in the first-half.

Things couldn't have been going much better for us... we were flying. I felt myself I was on my game. I felt every time I got the ball, I could cause these guys trouble. You get games like that sometimes and spells like that where everything goes for you. When you are on it, especially as a winger, you just want the ball all of the time. You just want to be involved and get on that ball.

As a winger, of course, you can also be isolated at times in a game and the ball might be going down one side and you are reliant on guys getting the ball out to you. But I was in the zone that night and I was playing well. I just wanted to get at the full-back the whole time.

We wouldn't have changed our system up too much going into Europe. It was... *we're at home here... let's play to our strengths.*

My main job was to get the ball and get at that full-back, test him, and get crosses into the box... and if I could get on the end of a cross or two myself, and try and nick a goal. Playing on the wing is hard work, not just going forward as you are expected to be tracking back and get back to help defensively as well. That was your job, and you knew what you had to do.

When things start off well and you just get in that zone, the confidence flows and you are *going*. As a winger when that happens, you want to make the most of it. I just wanted to run at them as much as I could.

You get a feel for the game as you go along. Sometimes you can be on the backfoot, and you are tracking and working back most of the time. That is hard work and mentally the drain it can have, maybe more so in away games when you are under pressure. At home you might think you can open up a bit more and get at teams. Away, as I learnt as we went along, you might have to play a little bit more defensively.

We had Kyiv on the rack, and we were pushing forward. We were 2-0 up at half-time and thinking *can we nick another one and can we really put this tie to bed*. Unfortunately, we didn't manage to get a third and then that killer goal in the 92nd minute from a corner. It was probably the turning point in the whole tie.

It gave them a little boost going back to their place, only one goal in it... and away goals then! In general, I don't think it should have taken the gloss off of a really good performance from us on the night.

When you sign for City and you are there for a while, you hear about the stories of the Bayern Munich games and Galatasaray... all of those games. They are the type of games that you want to be involved in. You are thinking, especially when we were 2-0 up against CSKA Kyiv, *If you could beat these who could we get in the next round?*

It is not easy to win games in Europe, it really isn't. In my career I think I was playing in my first six seasons where we qualified for Europe and never got past a round. So, you might win the first leg and get beaten in the second leg or draw. But over the two legs, we never managed to get through.

It is really difficult to do and especially the way the competitions were structured then. If you lost you were out, whereas it is a bit easier now to get a bit more experience the way it is structured. Back then, it was all or nothing.

To win those European games was special and to win them in Turner's Cross in front of the home crowd... they were right up for it as well, it is a special place to play. Any player up and down the League of Ireland will tell you, when you are playing in those European nights, they are really, *really* memorable. It doesn't come around that often and it is difficult. But again, that is where you measure yourself as a player.

That is where the clubs are looking to measure themselves too, and push their name out there, get more than just national coverage by getting across Europe... and pushing the club's name out there... Cork City mixing it with the big boys. That is what the club wants and obviously the prize money and everything that goes with these European runs, it can be vital to any League of Ireland club.

You can't underestimate how big it is, not just for players, but the whole club and the city of Cork as well to be competing on the European stage is amazing. The fans and everyone loves it, not just the players. For all the awards that are on offer, everyone wants to play in Europe.

That is really where you measure the progress of the league as a whole, seeing are teams getting through rounds and how are they progressing.

There is a lot riding on it. I was lucky to play in Europe 41 times in the end with the various clubs I was at. I was really lucky. You just can't beat it and it is extra special.

That was strange when we were going to Kyiv, and it was still in the zone around Chernobyl and the nuclear disaster that happened there. We actually brought our own chef and brought bottled water, to make sure we weren't using the water in the showers. In the hotel we were in, we took all the precautions.

We were just saying you couldn't take any chances. Even if you are on the training pitch, you might pick a piece of grass up… don't do any of that stuff. So, it was strange in that way

We prepared well. The big thing is, and it is something I've learned as you go along, there is a big difference playing home and away in European football. Some of the teams come to Turner's Cross, Tolka Park or wherever, and they are happy enough just to sit in and take a draw, confident that they will beat you at home.

You can get a false sense of security, maybe. I am not saying we underestimated Kyiv, but we were thinking… *if we can play this way again, we can take these.* But it is a totally different ball game.

The travel and everything, sometimes you are playing in a lot warmer conditions. On the night of the second leg we weren't great to be honest. I don't think we were hanging on as such, but we never really got at them or troubled them. They went and beat us 2-0 to go through.

A funny memory from the second leg… I was coming off the pitch and the next thing, the MC at the stadium was like *'number seven… number seven'* and I just thought it was the Kyiv number seven.

The next thing someone came over and pulled me aside, with the MC going *'Number seven… you were the best player'*. They handed me this big stereo system for being the best Cork City player over the two legs.

Here I am walking back into the dressing-room in Kyiv, and we were all disappointed after losing and being knocked out of the tie, with me carrying this big ghetto blaster thing. It is funny looking back on it now, but it probably wasn't too funny at the time because we were really disappointed. But it was nice to get that as well.

After the first leg, the CSKA Kyiv manager actually picked me and one or two of the other lads out and queried were we international players? He thought the standard and the way we played in the first leg... he couldn't believe that we weren't playing international football

When you are on that stage and measuring yourself against the best players, to hear that from an opposition manager is nice. But that was weird coming off that pitch in Kyiv with that stereo. It is something you can look back at now and laugh at. I loved my time there at Cork City and I had six really good years. I suppose the one thing you'd look back on and go... *we should have won a league title!* That is one thing that sticks with me, even now.

A league title with City, with the squad we had... I think we deserved one. I had a great time down in Cork and have great memories winning. Obviously winning the FAI Cup and we won the League Cup as well.

Turner's Cross is a brilliant place to play football when it is going well, with a packed house and the fans are great. Weren't so great when I returned playing for Shels and other teams! But when they are with you and supporting you down in Cork, it is huge and a great place to play.

Everyone knows you in the city and they really do get behind you. Cork City deserve success and you'd be hopeful they can come back up to the Premier Division because they should be there and the League of Ireland needs them. I have nothing but good memories from my time there.

We had a really good team and some really good players. We had a good mix. We had lads that were Cork City through and through... Dave Barry, Declan Daly, John Caulfield. We had Liam Murphy, Patsy Freyne... what a player!

Then we had a few young lads mixed in like myself and Colin O'Brien, and Greg O'Halloran was coming through as well. We had a really good mix, and we were a really good side. It was just a pity that we didn't bring a league title back.

Dave Barry was great. He understood the club inside out. Everyone loved him and all the fans loved him. He really focused on us and on our strengths; he tried to push us and get the best out of us. That was the type of guy that he was, getting onto lads to push themselves to give more.

Dave and Liam Murphy worked well together. The one big thing they had was that they played for the club, and they knew what the club needed and what the club wanted, along with the fan-base and everything.

They had the club's best interests at heart. They just wanted success and they were desperate for success for the team and for the city. When they came in, you were fully aware that is what they wanted and expected.

We used to train in Ballincollig and Ballinhassig, local parks and stuff which wasn't ideal. At the time you thought it could be better than this and should be better than this. But at the end of the day, that was the dynamic of things down there.

Most League of Ireland clubs then would have struggled to have their own training grounds and proper facilities. So that was difficult at times for them.

But they demanded the best from the players, and I think it was a pretty successful time. We qualified for Europe every season I was there, bar the last one. I think that Liam and Dave got them back on track and on the right trajectory, putting the club back up where it should be.

They deserve huge credit for that.

The year I left, my first game for Shels was Cork City away. That was the first game for George O'Callaghan and John O'Flynn. They beat us 3-0… beat us well. We didn't know these lads coming back, but they were top, *top* players. They went on to have really good careers with City.

I made the decision to move away and looking back now, it was the right decision. But I have really fond memories and great memories from my time in Cork. I still have some really good buddies down there as well. I signed for Shels and was five years at Shels. It wasn't an easy decision; it was a very tough decision, actually. I was 26. I wanted to win things, and I wanted to look back and go… *I have won x amount of leagues.*

I just thought at the time that Cork didn't match the ambition that I had, to really push it and go, like… *are we going to go out and try and recruit a player from a Dublin club, to see if he would come down to Cork and play.*

I don't know if they actively did that or were getting turned down. Or maybe that wasn't part of the make-up of the club at the time. I had some great experiences after, a European run with Shels and everything. It definitely was the right decision, but it wasn't an easy decision at the time.

It was a decision I felt I had to make for my career.

Now looking back, I know it was the right decision because I won five League of Ireland titles when I left, and a Setanta Cup with Drogheda United as well. I did ponder over it for quite a while, however.

I have nothing but good memories and good things to say about the club and the lads I played with. Cork is a hotbed of football, and it deserves success.

GEORGE O'CALLAGHAN

CORK CITY 3 ★ SHELBOURNE 0
League Of Ireland Premier Division
Turner's Cross
JULY 5, 2002

George O'Callaghan celebrates after scoring against Waterford in 2005.

★ **CORK CITY:** M Devine; A Carey, N Horgan, G Cronin, S Napier, M Mulconroy, C T O'Brien, A Bennett, J O'Flynn, **G O'Callaghan**, D Warren.

★ **SHELBOURNE:** S Williams; O Heary, B Prendeville, D Crawley, K Doherty, S Byrne, O Cahill, T Molloy, D Byrne, S Geoghegan, R Baker. Subs: J Gannon for Doherty, D Roberts for Geoghegan, W Hoolahan for Baker.

THE ACTION

NEW CORK CITY signings George O'Callaghan and John O'Flynn marked their debuts with goals which helped the Leesiders to a sizzling start to the season against champions Shelbourne.

The pair combined for the City opener in the 15th minute. Alan Bennett played the ball out to Michael Mulconroy, who chipped the ball into the path of O'Flynn. The former Peterborough youngster continued the attack with an inch perfect cross for O'Callaghan to finish courtesy of a right footed volley to the corner.

The home side extended their advantage two minutes before half-time. After Bennett won a header to set O'Flynn away, he showed deft footwork to break and subsequently slot the ball beyond the grasp of Steve Williams in the Shelbourne goal.

To top off an evening they would rather forget, Shels had Trevor Molloy sent off shortly after the interval.

City for their part capped off a comprehensive evening with a third goal in the 77th minute. O'Flynn was on hand to plant the ball into the bottom corner, after racing onto a pass from Colin T O'Brien.

Overall, City's new look team were fully deserving winners over the Dublin side, who included Ollie Cahill lining out against his former club.

★★★★★

66

IT WAS THE start of summer football in the League of Ireland. Shelbourne were the best team in the league and they had all the best players... Ollie Cahill, Owen Heary and all these guys. We turned up that Friday night against Shels, who had just won the league.

It was our first league game against them. I was after coming home, and John O'Flynn (Flynny) was after coming home. Flynny crossed the ball to me after 15 minutes and I got a volley, my first goal in front of the Shed. I think that put a whole mark on the club that night.

It made the hype about the whole club build up. The Shed was packed... and we were scoring goals. We were exciting to watch at home. It really gave that buzz around the city, that we were ready to be contenders again and try to win the league.

You had a lot of lads who had gone to England and came back. I suppose we all felt like we had failed over in the UK. Then we came back and, all of a sudden, you are playing for Cork City, and you obviously get the media attention. When I was playing for Port Vale, you are not in *The Sun*, *The Mirror* or *The Daily Star* over there in the UK. Then, all of a sudden, all of these papers are taking interest in you.

I came back from playing with Port Vale in the English Championship, which is a very good league... some top teams. I always remember our first game was against Bantry Gunners down in West Cork and it was up a hill on the worst pitch possible. At half-time it was 0-0 and I always remember Mick Devine and Patsy Freyne having a smoke. I wasn't used to that culture.

It was a big shock for me and, at the time, we only had four full professionals. I think it was myself, Flynny, Conor O'Grady and Greg O'Halloran. The four of us were training with Liam Murphy (Murph) out on the Tramore Road... four of us on a hurling pitch doing drills, waiting to go to training that night.

So, it was a big, *big* culture shock for me.

Anyone who ever watched me play in those years around 2003 and '04... I think I was a bit reckless because I was after coming back from the UK, and I felt that was it! I had the chance to go to Arsenal and Tottenham, and then I ended up basically leaving Port Vale on really bad terms.

Back home, I just felt like I was playing on Friday nights with my mates. We had that environment at Cork City, where you had great lads like Greg O'Halloran and Conor O'Grady. We all built up a relationship… more of a friendship, rather than lads in a professional football club. That kind of went on the whole season, where we all stuck together.

As it progressed, we got better and better as things grew.

In the week leading up to that game, it was all the hype about Shelbourne and they were going to beat us three or four nil. I think that game gave us all the confidence to realise that we were good enough to play in the League of Ireland and that we had a team that could compete.

Shelbourne had the best players and the best paid players. That night we blew them away and I think it gave them a shock. We spent the next two or three seasons fighting with Shelbourne to win the league. But I will never forget that first game against them… and Declan Daly and Stephen Napier in the changing room.

They were two unbelievable blokes and two solid lads. It was just like, their team talk before we went out was like a war cry. They had us wired to the moon. We were ready to go and it was like going to war. It is like when you watch the British and Irish Lions now and you see these documentaries and lads making these speeches.

That is what it was like. It reminded me when I was younger of my GAA days because I wasn't used to that in the UK, where it is… *just go out and play.* This meant something and with Decky and Stephen Napier it was just amazing.

What used to burn inside me… and I love Pat Morley he is a great guy, but Pat used to say he was the best No 10 that played for Cork City. So, my thing then in games or in seasons was to show that I was better than Pat Morley… and I was a better No 10. Anytime I used to score or get a goal, I used to text Pat and sign off… *'from the best No 10 at Cork City'.*

It was amazing because I grew up going to Cork City, going to the Shed and watching the games… seeing Decky, seeing Stephen Napier. Morley was gone and John Caulfield was gone. All of a sudden, you are in the dressing-room with all of these and, I suppose, the closest thing you'd get to Patsy Freyne from the Northside is probably me. Patsy gave me great advice all down through the years.

If I needed advice, Patsy was there for me. He used to tell me how to get through games and how to deal with the League of Ireland and what to do. Those guys were legends in my eyes and my heroes. So, for me to be in the same room as them and play on a pitch with them was amazing. I suppose it is a Cork thing in us, that we all want to believe and want to be better than others.

We all have that competitive edge. I think that came in and we decided that myself and Flynny wanted to be better than Morley and Caulfield.

When I moved back into midfield, I wanted to be better than Patsy or Davy Barry. I think that burning desire and competitive edge really came in. But in saying that, Davy Barry, Patsy and Pat Morley... they were always there for advice and to help you improve. I mean, they are honestly great guys.

What I also remember about that match was, I came home from England and I had no football boots. I was going through Blackpool at half five to play in this game against Shelbourne, the best team in the league. I had to ring my brother saying... 'I am absolutely broke, is there any chance you could buy me some football boots'.

He went into Cummins Sports in Blackpool and he bought me Preds. It was the hard ground, so you needed moulded studs. But my brother John came out and gave me metal studs. I went into the changing room with these white boots and everyone was like 'how are you going to play with metal studs, the ground is rock hard'. I was like 'I'll be grand'.

My brother bought my first pair of boots when I went to Port Vale. Whatever happened, there was a little bit of magic in them that night anyway. I scored a good volley in the first 15 minutes. I used those boots for the rest of the season... I didn't care if it was raining or sunny.

That was the first time I had played in Turner's Cross since I was about 14. I literally just had an argument with all of the Shels players for the whole match.

'If ye are the best players in this league, it is embarrassing!' I was telling them. That was the start of my hate-love relationship with Shels.

It put a black mark on me for the Shelbourne lads because, from that day on, it was me and Shelbourne fighting constantly for the next four or five years while I was in the League of Ireland. I think that first game against Shelbourne and their reaction, how they acted with us, I think that set the fuse for us to go... *we are coming for you!*

Obviously, we had bumps in the road, but we were ready for them. The League of Ireland is a tough league because it is full of very honest lads. I think a lot of lads come over from England thinking it is going to be easy, but it is not. You have got to be one hundred percent committed in the League of Ireland or else you will get found out.

I think we were all starting to learn how to play in the league, just to have that little bit of know-how about the league. Knowing what to do at corners and slowing down free kicks... going down in the last five minutes to waste some time. Shelbourne had that, but we all needed to learn that and it took us a good two or three years to get that.

There is so much more pressure playing for Cork City when you are a Cork lad. You realise when you come to Cork, you have all your family and all your friends there.

So, you are under pressure to perform. It came to the stage where you knew where everybody was sitting. For me, playing for Cork City was the most pressure I had because I knew I *had* to perform. I think there was a lot more pressure playing at City then playing with any other club.

I don't think Murph gets the credit that he deserves because, at the end of the day, it is better to be a lucky manager than a good manager. When you think of standout names in Cork City... Murph brought in Flynny, Dan Murray, Alan Reynolds... and he brought Billy Woods back. He brought me back... he brought Dave Warren back. That is a good scouting network and I think the club wish they had the current scouting network now.

I will never forget what Murph did for me.

I remember him signing me in Clancy's and bringing in a euro converter. I never think he gets the credit because people are down on Murph, but if you look back at some of the players he brought in, there were some very good players. Pat Dolan didn't know his luck when he came to Cork City. We'd played against St Pat's when Pat was there. I think he saw the ability that we had and the players that we had. It just needed guidance and discipline.

But as I said, it is better to be a lucky manager. When Pat came in and did that, it changed the whole culture of the club. Murph put the bones in for that foundation for all of those players to come through.

There was plenty of times in that season where he should have dropped me or left me out. But he always stuck by me and because I was playing week-in and week-out, it kind of grew my confidence. We played off the cuff. Anyone who came to the home games, they could see we were capable of scoring four or five goals in every game.

Away from home it really found us out in 2003, because we didn't have the organisation or the discipline or the structure to really compete with the sides who were winning the league, like Shels and Bohs.

When Pat Dolan came in, we were very unlucky not to win the league in 2004. Then we went on to win the league in 2005 with Rico. I never appreciated it when I was there because I kind of felt a failure coming back from the UK. But then I got the chance to build.

I always used to say a decade of the rosary, asking and praying to God that I can be a Cork sports star. When you look back at 2003-05… I was that. I was up there with the Ronan O'Gara's, the Sean Og's… all of these sports stars. I loved Larry Tompkins and I feel that I got a taste of that… to be a sports star in Cork and knowing what it is like to be that. In the games I always played with pressure because I always wanted to go back to the UK… I wanted to sort out the demons in my head that I can get back and play to the standard that I was at.

We had a project that we were going to win the league within three years. We weren't on great money any of us, to be fair. We were on a quarter of what the top Shels or Bohemians lads were getting, but everyone in Ireland loves to play in Turner's Cross. Without doubt, we are the biggest club in Ireland.

I was offered contracts with Drogheda on €3,000 a week, Shels €2,500 a week, but I stayed with Cork on €650 a week because I wanted to win the league. I knew we had that goal set out and how much it meant to everyone in Cork… what needed to be done. I still think back on that team… if we had a bit more guidance and Murph had a bit more experience, we would have been up there fighting for that title.

The likes of Shamrock Rovers, they obviously have the history and all that, but I really believe if Pat Dolan wasn't sacked in 2004, that we would have kicked on with Cork City and got into the Champions League… selling out Páirc Uí Chaoimh instead of playing in Turner's Cross.

When Pat was there, I think that club would have been amazing. I think it would have been a completely different future for the whole club.

As I get older now, looking back it was one hundred percent the happiest time I was in football. We weren't a professional club, but it was a team spirit and a bond that I had with everyone. Some of my best friends still now are the likes of Flynny, Kearney, Dan Murray, Joey Gamble… all of these guys, we are all still very close.

That kind of team spirit that we had means a lot to me now. I just wish I appreciated it more when I was there.

DANNY MURPHY

CORK CITY 2 ★ WATERFORD UNITED 3
League Of Ireland Premier Division
Turner's Cross
APRIL 6, 2004

Danny Murphy in full flow with Cork City in 2013.

★ **CORK CITY:** M Devine; N Horgan, D Murray, W Byrne, **D Murphy**, C O'Brien, B Sweeney, G O'Callaghan, J O'Flynn, N Fenn, K Doyle. Subs: B Woods for Horgan, L Kearney for Murphy, M Nwankwo for Sweeney.

★ **WATERFORD UNITED:** D Connor; K O'Brien, D Breen, P Purcell, P Leahy, V Sullivan, A Reynolds, D Mulcahy, K Waters, W Bruton, D Murphy. Sub: M Clifford for Bruton.

THE ACTION

DESPITE GETTING OFF to the most perfect of starts in what was a rip-roaring contest, Cork City fell to defeat at the hands of their Munster rivals Waterford United at Turner's Cross.

City opened the scoring after just 18 seconds on the clock. From 20 yards out, Kevin Doyle was on hand to impressively slot the ball home following a cross by Colin O'Brien. Cork remained in control of proceedings until the 19th minute when Waterford got back on level terms.

Daryl Murphy stepped up and successfully converted from the penalty spot for the Blues, after Willie Bruton had been hauled down by Billy Woods in the box.

A few minutes later, however, and it was City who went back in front. Danny Murphy found the back of the net with a brilliant free kick, as the former QPR man's swerved his effort beyond the grasp of Dan Connor in the Waterford goal.

Kevin Waters equalised again for Blues in the 41st minute, with his shot deflecting into the net off Willie Byrne. That was before defender Pat Purcell then hit what turned out to be the Waterford winner in first-half stoppage time, stabbing home an Alan Reynolds' free-kick after being teed up by Bruton.

★★★★★

66

FOR ME, THIS game set out who I am and what you are going to get out of me, what you will see from me as a person and what you will see from me as a player.

I think that game made me the player that I was… made me the person who the fans, I felt, could look up to and could have high expectations of, just because they knew the way I played. That was the game that really stood out to me, letting everyone know… *this is the sort of player we've got.*

I always remember that Waterford game because I had scored in it as well and it was something for me that was like really intense… a great atmosphere. That game was really early in my City career, but for some reason it is a game that just stays with me, something I really enjoy to remember.

The game really made me realise what it was like to play for Cork City, what it meant to play for the club and the level you had to be at to play for Cork… what people expected of you week-in and week-out.

I think that is why, for me, this game made a massive difference. I wanted to win every game for Cork City and I just wanted to make sure if I didn't play well, I made it a living hell for someone I was playing against. Knowing what you had to do and what was expected of you, it was difficult to replicate at other places because you never really had that same feeling. Like you would go somewhere and it doesn't hurt enough when you are playing and not winning.

Whereas when I played for Cork, if I didn't win it bothered me. It didn't just last for that night, it would last for a few days. Whereas when I played with other clubs, it just never felt the same.

I knew what I had to produce every game and I knew the level of expectation as well. For me the actual physicality of the game, I really enjoyed it… how we had to play and the things we did. They were the things that stood out and I actually played quite well in that game. I had a little battle with Alan Reynolds and I didn't back down from him. He had a personality… he was always going to be aggressive and be physical. Not everyone enjoyed that side of the game. That, for me, was probably a big part of my game.

I just remember standing over the ball and it was a wide free kick. I was looking at Dan Connor in the Waterford goal and he thought I was going to cross it. I saw him trying to nick a few yards to go the other way and I decided…

I am actually going to hit this at the near post.

I caught it really well and it went straight in.

Everyone knows what Dan Connor was like as a player. When he was at Waterford, how he used to wind up the Cork City fans and stuff like that. I was like… *I will shut him up straight away.* I just remember that very clearly.

I remember the build-up to the game too, and how hyped up it was. Pat Dolan was good at doing that and he made it a big thing. It was a good atmosphere and a proper derby game. As the seasons went on, you didn't have a whole lot of derby games with Waterford, but you had games with the likes of Shels and Shamrock Rovers.

At that stage, Waterford were more of a rival for us and it was more of a bigger game. But as we developed as a team and got better, then we had other rival games with some of the bigger clubs and they took over and became more important.

All of that year in 2004, all of the build-up and all the work that Pat Dolan did, it literally set us up to come into the next season and go on to win the title. We were just well structured and well organised. He had built a team of some really good players. We added Joe Gamble and a couple of others as the season went on.

We just got better players coming in and it made us a stronger team… a better footballing side. I think we had an okay season in 2004 and we finished second under Pat. But it was really set up for the next season.

I think all of the work we did on and off the pitch in 2004, in terms of the European run and some of the results we picked up that year, that set us up.

We were very well organised under Pat, but as we added players we became a better footballing team and more of a threat. Pat put a structure in place and he made it very professional. He made it more of a professional club and outfit, in terms of how you trained and the level you had to train at.

He put those things in place, and he took it away from being a semi-professional club… whereas we were now training nearly every day. Training was very intense with Pat, he got us very fit and we ran quite a lot.

That is the way we played and that is what made us the team we were, building us as characters as well. Pat had a couple of set pieces that he liked to work on and we used them quite a lot. He was well organised, with everything in his little pad down to a tee and how he wanted his team to exactly look.

I think we were training three mornings a week and then we would do an afternoon with the part-time boys. So, the younger players were in full-time more or less… with the part-time boys coming in for the evenings.

Them little structures made a big difference for us. I think that was the biggest thing and I think that is what people very rarely forget, our back four probably never changed. It was me, Dan Murray, Alan Bennett and Neal Horgan.

We all knew each other's game really well. We played really well with each other, so that for me was one of the biggest things… that consistency of the same back four, over and over again. If you look at some of the best teams in the world, the back four very rarely changes. I think that we had really strong characters. We were a really close group and just got on really well with each other.

But we also pushed the boundaries with each other because we would constantly be winding each other up. Messing around… anyone coming in with bad gear would get terrorised, putting ice in people's socks and shoes. Stuff like that, and constant jokes. I think that was why we did so well, because everyone fought for each other. We knew when to get serious and when it was time to not joke about.

What Pat Dolan did, it made a massive impact… the things he put in place. I know Rico (Damien Richardson) would say it himself, he just came in and said 'Do you know what, you are good enough'. He literally just cut the handcuffs off. Pat had us very structured and organised. Maybe at certain times we were a little bit restricted, because we played a certain way. Rico more or less came in and said, 'No, ye can do this!'

The first time that I met him was as a left back, and I remember him saying to me that he wanted me to get up and down the pitch, not just playing left back. It just added more to my game and it gave me the freedom to be a little bit more expressive in how I played. He gave you that trust and it made a big difference for me personally going forward.

Any game at Turner's Cross was like having an extra player. The fans always knew how to get you through a game. When you weren't playing well or doing well, you knew about it. But when you are firing and… like the European nights, when you tired and were up against it, they'd get you through a game. So, it was good as a stadium, and atmosphere… it was always excellent.

I didn't know a whole lot about the club. Then I came and played the Dublin City game at home and the atmosphere was amazing. Then you had the Waterford game and I was thinking this is something special, this could be really good. That literally just kick-started it for me and I wanted to be a part of it. I was heavily invested in it.

I think Cork City was where my best football was played really. It was always something for me that will always be a big part of my life. When you win and are successful at Cork, people really look after you.

Everyone wants to say hello and get to know you. For me, it is nice, even times now when I go back, people still come up to you and still have an interest in what you are doing. It is good and it is something you will never get anywhere else. I will never forget the intensity of playing there and what it meant to play for Cork City. For me, it is something I always carried on, any club I go to now as a coach… I try to build that kind of atmosphere. That is what I try to do and it is really hard to replicate.

I think the expectation of people in Cork, anyway, is no matter what sport you play in, they want to be the best at it. It is just a Cork thing, isn't it… where it is expected. It is not something that they want, it is something that they *expect*.

I still look out for the results. I still have contacts with some of the boys there and I still speak to them on occasions. Cork City is always something that I will pay attention to and that I always will be looking out for. I always want to know how they are doing, who is playing and who is not playing.

I will always have a vested interest in Cork City Football Club.

LIAM KEARNEY

MALMÖ FF 0 ★ CORK CITY 1
UEFA Intertoto Cup First Round Second Leg
(Cork City won 4–1 on aggregate)
Malmö Stadion
JUNE 27, 2004

Liam Kearney weaves his way through Nantes on another big European night for Cork City in 2004.

★ **MALMÖ FF:** M Asper; D Majstorovic, O Persson, P Andersson, H Mattisson, A Alves, T Olsson, J I Hoiland, J Elanga, D Lukanovic, N Skoog. Subs: G Holgersson for Andersson, J Jonsson for Elanga, T Grahn for Mattisson.

★ **CORK CITY:** M Devine; C Lordan, A Bennett, D Murray, D Murphy, K Doyle, C O'Brien, G O'Callaghan, **L Kearney**, N Fenn, J O'Flynn. Subs: D Behan for Doyle, B Woods for O'Flynn.

70

THE ACTION

IT WAS ONE of the greatest ever European nights for Cork City Football Club, as they defeated Sweden's Malmö FF away from home in the UEFA Intertoto Cup.

The victory on the night and over both legs was no more than what City deserved, as they played with a passion and a swagger throughout.

Malmö's best opportunity in the first-half came after 40 minutes, when striker Nicklas Skoog hit a free kick from the edge of the penalty area over the bar.

City took the lead on the night shortly before the hour mark. From a cross by Neale Fenn into the box, Liam Kearney was on hand to tuck the ball away with a crisp finish from 15 yards out.

With Malmö now needing three goals, Alfonso Alves went close with an effort that went just wide of the post, while Michael Devine denied Majstorovic after 70 minutes when he powered a header towards goal.

City also continued to attack with confidence and John O'Flynn fired over the bar with a great effort from 30 yards after 82 minutes.

Alves hit the bar for Malmö with a long range effort late on in the contest. But at the end of the night and this tie on aggregate, Cork City stood tall to record one of their greatest ever European victories.

★★★★★

66

IT WAS A huge result for the club, and it is still one of the biggest results in Europe that Cork City have had.

I just remember it was a long clearance and Flynny won the header. Neale Fenn found a pocket of space and he crossed. I was coming in at the back post and I remember the ball just fell nicely… and I volleyed into the bottom corner. It was a special moment in my career and a special moment for the club.

It was nice to be part of a team that was able to win games like that.

We were probably exhausted after the amount of work that we put into the game, because in Europe there is so much work done without the ball. You must keep yourself organised, stop the gaps for them to be creating opportunities. If any player switches off in a European game and give the opposition one chance, then it is generally a goal.

The biggest thing I always remember about European games, and Malmö as well, is that you just had to be constantly and mentally tuned in. You could not be out of position at the wrong time because you knew it would come back on you if there was an opportunity given for a goal. I'd say at the end of the game we were exhausted, but delighted.

It kind of instilled this mentality of how you dealt with a big game and how you prepared for it. Even the day of a big game, how you rested and staying in hotels. Just getting used to that footballers life, really. If definitely stood us in good stead for the following year, when we had games where the pressure was on us. We had to go to the last game to win the league in 2005, which we should have won a long time before that. I think it stood to us one hundred percent.

We went to Nijmegen and Nantes, and the following year it was Djurgårdens. So, it was a great time for the club and it was great to be a part of it. Pat Dolan instilled huge confidence and belief in all of us. A lot of us were young players who had been to England and had come back for whatever reason. But we just kind of came together at a very special time. There was a lot of talent and a lot of good players.

Everyone was probably eager to prove that they had a future as a professional footballer. You are talking about really talented players who just came together at the right time. Under Pat, we could compete in Europe.

NEC Nijmegen were a Dutch Premier Division team and to go through against them was another huge achievement in itself. I think over there, it was such a workmanlike performance, we never worked so hard to get the 0-0 over there... and it was 1-0 to us at home.

When you look back on it, it was a really an exciting time. We probably never fully appreciated how amazing that time was. But it is nice to watch back the footage and to see how well we did. We weren't just beating the lesser European teams, we were beating top teams which was great to do. It was nice to be a part of it. Hopefully, we will have a lot more of those nights to come again.

Those kind of memories, you will never forget. How much it meant to the club, myself and my family. They can never be taken away, they are always going to be remembered. I still get people asking me and coming up to me talking about that goal. You'll always at times meet people... even the Malmö hotel manager who never forgot it.

I think any time that you travel on a bus or that you stay overnight somewhere, you are always going to improve the team bonding situation. You are around the players and are travelling back together after the game. It is a huge part of it. It builds that team spirit and environment, and you bond a lot closer than you might do if you just go into training and go home every day.

We were all similar ages back then, so we probably had a lot more in common than sometimes when you go into a dressing-room with older and younger players... some people in one corner and others in the other. We were all very quite close back then. That definitely helped on the pitch, because we weren't shy in giving our opinion to each other at times, which is important as well.

The feeling of... *we know now we can compete at this level, and we have proven it, let's keep this run going.* It just backed up the belief that Pat Dolan had put into us.

Pat Dolan really resurrected Cork City for me. He came in and he cleared out all the drinking culture as much as he could. It was all a professional attitude and a professional system, and players understood that if you are playing for Cork City, then these are the standards that you needed to live by or you would be out the door very quickly. Pat, personally for me when I came back from England, he rebuilt my career as well. He gave me the confidence to make a career for myself in the League of Ireland.

I owe Pat a lot in terms of what he did for me. His man-management was superb. All Pat wanted was to try to provide the best for us, to give us every opportunity to do well. When we went over to Europe, he brought a big squad and made sure everybody was part of it. We all gained huge experience as well at a young age.

That is the main thing for players in Ireland, if they get the opportunity to finish in the top three in the league, generally you are going to get a chance to play in Europe. It was a huge opportunity for us. To go from one country to the next country in a week, knowing that if you win you are going again the next Wednesday.

It was really exciting. We were just at the point that we were going… *where are we next week?*

The football, it was nice to play at that stage where it is a different type of a game to say in England or Ireland. So, you had to be able to take care of the football and technically be good to retain the ball. We had players like that, and we had a lot of players who went onto play at a higher level again after that.

I have a funny story of a fella who is running the hotel up in Galway now, the Galmont Hotel. He is a massive Malmö fan. He had been working in Galway and came down to watch the first game. He still says to me that we just expected to walk all over ye, and that Malmö are a massive club. He said he couldn't believe we had beaten them over there as well.

It was a team that I was lucky to be a part of, where we felt at that level, we had the players technically and tactically that we could compete with them. I think that just instilled the belief going over away from home… I think we were the first Irish side to go away from home and beat a Swedish team at the time.

We all knew each other's strengths and we knew each other's qualities. We made the best of it and I think after six, seven, eight months, we all gelled very well together. We built towards that 2005 title-winning season from already having the 2004 season together. There were top players in that squad and I think everyone carried out their roles and responsibilities fairly well.

I came from Conna in East Cork and, before I went to England, I would have been big into the GAA and hurling especially. When I came back from England, I was looking for a club and I obviously would have known of Cork City. Once I met Pat Dolan and saw what he wanted to do with the club and where he wanted to take it, I was very lucky he brought me in and gave me my opportunity.

I think I was probably in my prime to a point. I felt as good as I ever did as a footballer. Full of confidence, and I knew I was playing with a lot of talented players who worked well together back then. There were other memorable times… in 2007 we won the cup. That was a nice thing to do, having thrown it away in 2005. It was important to do that.

It was certainly one of the most exciting times to be a player at Cork City. I was lucky I had Danny Murphy behind me at left back. Me and Danny had a very good understanding of the game together. Even if Danny was marauding down the left wing, I knew I was going to sit in and keep the defensive shape for him.

Danny came to Cork very similar to me. He had left QPR and we actually played against each other in the under-19 Premier League final. I would have played with Danny as well with Ireland underage. So, we had a little bit of history together that way. When you talk about Mick Devine… he was a super goalkeeper. We had Dan Murray, Alan Bennett, Derek Coughlan! Look at Neal Horgan… what a career he had as well. We certainly knew going forward that we had a good base behind us.

You talk about really good lads and I'd class a lot of them still as my friends.

We built up a real big fan-base at that time just by how well we were doing. For me, the best games I always loved to be involved in were the European games. I thought it was really a test to show where you were at as a player. Because technically you were going to be tested, physically they were going to be testing you.

But also, you'd have time on the ball to show what type of footballer you really were, because sometimes in the League of Ireland it is so up and down and a hundred miles an hour, that it can be very difficult sometimes to show your capabilities. European games for me were the biggest highlight.

I always loved the big games as well, cup semi-finals… and the Derry game turned out to be nearly a cup final that we had to win, to win the league. So, kind of big pressured occasions, I used to look forward to.

That is where you challenge yourself. Since 2004, there has been huge results in the League of Ireland. If you look at Shamrock Rovers getting to the group stages, Dundalk getting to the group stages. There is progression to be seen there. Are they overachieving with budgets one hundred percent? We are still nowhere near the level of investment to get to a consistent basis of getting into the Europa League. But at the same time, it just shows the talent that is here.

You could go through the amount of players in the Irish squad who have come through the League of Ireland. Now you look at international teams underage, and they are full of League of Ireland academy players

I have been a coach and a player, so now I am overseeing things as the Cork City Head Of Academy. I have been lucky that Colin Healy was the original Head. I have a good relationship with Colin and if there are any questions or anything, he is very good to help me with them.

I have enjoyed it. There is some serious talent coming through the club. It is my job to make sure we have a flow of players, if possible. If there are players we can sell, then that is another option as well. It has been good. I am probably not on the pitch as much as I would have liked. But it is an important role to do and I am glad to be doing it.

Over my time playing and coaching, I certainly have a good grasp of how things can escalate, how the crowds can come in if you are really doing well.

If things are done right and the backing is there in terms of investment, there is no bigger club in Ireland than Cork City.

KEVIN DOYLE

CORK CITY FC 1 ★ NEC NIJMEGAN 0
UEFA Intertoto Cup Second Round Second Leg
Turner's Cross
JULY 11, 2004

Kevin Doyle beats Jose Valencia of NEC Nijmegen to the ball to score the winning goal in the Intertoto cup in 2004.

★ **CORK CITY:** M Devine, C Lordan, A Bennett, D Murray, D Murphy, C O'Brien, G O'Callaghan, L Kearney, **K Doyle**, N Fenn, J O'Flynn Sub: K Murray for Fenn.

★ **NEC NIJMEGEN:** D Gentenaar; R Wielaert, P Pothuizen, A Ebbinge, J Valencia; B Van der Doelen, P Heije, Tininho, S Boutahar, R Denneboom, F Demouge. Subs: P Wisgerhof for Pothuizen, A Prent for Valencia, J Simr for Heije.

THE ACTION

A 47th MINUTE GOAL from Kevin Doyle was enough to secure a memorable European victory for Cork City over Dutch side NEC Nijmegen. This was another iconic and well deserved win for City in continental action in 2004 under the management of Pat Dolan.

Roared on by a fantastic home support on a sunny evening at a sold-out Turner's Cross, in the first-half City goalkeeper Michael Devine saved well at the feet of Romano Dennenboom. While at the other end, Dennis Gentenaar saved from a Liam Kearney header, as City were not overawed one bit by their opposition.

City struck with the decisive blow early into the second-half. George O'Callaghan provided the cross into the penalty area and Doyle jumped highest to head the ball into the back of the net. The Rebel Army went close to extending their lead, but John O'Flynn was denied by Gentenaar in the Nijmegen goal.

City continued to push and Gentenaar again saved from an O'Flynn header, while a Doyle shot went the wrong side of the post. Nijmegen threw everything at it to get an equaliser, but the City defence, especially Dan Murray and Alan Bennett, were rock solid.

Michael Devine produced a fine save in injury time to deny substitute Alexander Prent, as Cork City held on for another historic victory in Europe. This result saw City progress into the third round of the UEFA Intertoto Cup and set up a meeting with French outfit FC Nantes.

★★★★★

66

THE GAME THAT stands out for me would be when we played NEC Nijmegen at home in the UEFA Intertoto Cup. We played really well and, from a personal point of view, I scored. But we won the game and we deserved to win as well. We had a fabulous bunch of players. It was a full house and a sunny day.

We matched them, against a club that would have been in terms of facilities and budget, way ahead of us. But we were as good or better than them and beat them. Personally, getting on the scoresheet as well gave me a lot of confidence. It made me realise we can play against anyone on our day and beat them… satisfying and confidence-boosting.

NEC Nijmegen were playing in the Dutch League and doing quite well. So, it gave all of us in that team a big confidence boost… we went on then and won the League of Ireland the next year. I think we beat Malmö before that. But that summer… there was a spell where we won some big games. I remember Turner's Cross was sold out for all of them.

I have a picture of the Nijmegan goal, so my memory is quite clear of it. I think my mother has a picture up in the house. My memory of it was, I think, I was playing on the wing… I don't think I was playing centre-forward.

Someone swung the ball into the box, I think it was George O'Callaghan… and I was thinking that I was going to be given a free against me.

That is my memory, thinking I scored a header… but I was up above a fella on his shoulders basically heading the ball in. I remember thinking… *the ref is going to give a free here for this.* It wasn't a foul, but he didn't jump and I did. So, it looked as if I was after getting a boost up on his shoulders and seeing the ball go into the bottom corner.

Pat Dolan was managing at the time. He'd have boosted us up to be superstars and way better than them. We would have known everything about all their players. He would have had a dossier done on Nijmegen. So we would have really been drilled… drilled into us that we were as good as them or better than them, and deserved to beat them. So, we had no fear. It was strange those games that time.

I think the Cork City fans thought we should win those games or believed we could win them as well. The club was in a good spot at the time regarding players… our squad and the support that we used to get. We always went into games thinking we were going to win them.

Pat Dolan's best quality was not making you feel inferior, trying to boost you up to make you feel the best player in the world at that time… that Cork City was as good as any club in Europe. That we had a right to be there and should win.

It wasn't a case of going there to enjoy the game. He put a lot of pressure on us to win those games… and not winning wasn't good enough.

So that was how he managed us. We had good facilities, we trained in good places and we stayed in good hotels. Everything was done so that we didn't feel inferior in any way. I think that was a real strong point from Pat.

Going to somewhere like Nijmegen, Malmö or Nantes, places like that where they have better stadiums… I suppose you could feel you don't belong. But we certainly didn't feel like that when Pat was managing us.

I vaguely remember getting interviewed by national journalists, that you maybe normally wouldn't get interviewed by. I remember people that would have not really known about my League of Ireland career, and all of a sudden seeing and reading about it, taking notice. That was the same for all of the squad.

Those games too, from a League of Ireland perspective, gave us a lot more confidence and a feeling that we were the best team in the country. There can be a lot taken from those games if they go well.

Why this game means so much to me? We beat a really good team and I scored. It sort of broke a barrier in my brain that I could do this from a professional point of view going forward.

That I felt good enough in this game and was playing well… that I could go on and have a good career as a footballer. That was sort of a mental barrier maybe I broke in that game from a personal point of view.

So that is why it stands out in my mind. I still have a picture of me sitting on a fella's back and seeing the ball head back into the far corner.

I was young and full of confidence. I used to play on the right wing when I first went to Cork for the first season and a half, or two seasons. It was only in that last bit of the league-winning season, the first 10 games when I starting moving up front. Much of the time I was between wing and up front, depending on who was fit or not. With the list of strikers that we had, there was a lot of competition for places to play centre-forward.

So when I did go up front, I got on a good run of form and started to score a lot of goals. When things are going well, it makes it very easy. I had good players around me though to help me. I played up front with the likes of Neale Fenn… George O'Callaghan sort of moved into a central midfield role.

But we were a very attacking team. We had good wingers like Liam Kearney and Roy O'Donovan, who used to play right wing a lot of the time. We had players who made it very easy to be a centre-forward. Everything was exciting. It was about attacking football, creating chances and then whoever was up front trying to take them.

We always got good crowds at Cork when I was there anyway. So, this was just a little bit extra and you got more national attention, I suppose. The press were a bit more interested. It was a chance to show on a stage outside the League of Ireland, and if you are a young player who dreams of playing for the international team or moving across the water, it was a chance to show your ability and what level you might be at to test yourself as well.

That was a big plus of playing in those games. I know from my point of view, going and joining Reading, that was one of the reasons they went and signed me. They saw that I played well in those games and had a decent ability.

Not ideal for Cork City and Cork City fans, that players are trying to showcase themselves. But it is mutually beneficial, I suppose, we do well for ourselves and well for the club as well.

We were a professional full-time club. We trained no differently to any team in the world. We trained every morning. We had decent facilities and we didn't want for anything. There was good players, a young squad and an exciting squad.

When you go through the players on that team, I am not going to name them out because I will probably forget and miss someone… but if you go through that team and the subs even, with the quality we had, I might be slightly biased but I think that was as strong a League Of Ireland squad as you would have seen in a long, *long* time.

A GOOD FEW lads went on to get international caps from that Cork City squad. There are a lot of lads still playing from that squad and had long careers. There was fabulous ability.

John O'Flynn and George O'Callaghan were two who stood out for me when I signed for Cork, they were quality young players in the league and exciting young players.

That whole squad though… and just even from a centre-forwards or strikers perspective, there was Roy O'Donovan, myself, George O'Callaghan, John O'Flynn, Neale Fenn… Denis Behan as well. I don't know if I am leaving anyone out, but there was a real selection of players and really good players to choose from. Even getting in the team at the time was hard work.

We got great support. At the time, Turner's Cross and Cork was the best place to play in Ireland. The biggest club and the best support, a full-time club with the best players. At the time, I thought we were the biggest club, with the best setup. The best coverage from a press point of view, with the radio, the local newspapers and everything. We were treated correctly as professional footballers. At the time, I am trying to think… there was nowhere that could match Cork City for a full house… for crowds and for noise.

For everything that goes with being a professional footballer, it had it all at the time. As a young player, it meant that when I moved to England maybe a year later, it wasn't such a big jump for me mentally because I was used to playing in front of big crowds and dealing with pressure. Because there was *pressure* playing for Cork City. I think there was more pressure playing for Cork City maybe than some of the bigger clubs in Dublin, because it was more intense living in Cork.

Everyone knew about Cork City and the players and would be putting pressure on you play well and perform.

It prepared me anyway. It gave me a great grounding and learning experience to the life as a professional footballer. More probably the pressures that go with it. That is brilliant and what you want… to feel under pressure. You want every result to count, people to question you and support you brilliantly when things are going well.

That is what it was like at Cork City.

We were a really tight-knit group. We used to socialise together and do a lot of stuff together. We were young lads living in Cork. I was living on College Road, right in the thick of it for my two and a half or three years there. It was great fun and we had good camaraderie on and off the pitch at the time.

I played for St Pat's in Dublin who are a very good club. But it wouldn't have prepared me like Cork City did. As I said, the pressure... the local newspapers, the journalists, the local radio stations... the crowds at the game.

Everything at Cork City sort of prepared you in a slightly smaller scale, but still in a proper way for my future career. It meant that going to Reading wasn't nearly as daunting.

I'd done that at Cork City and played in big games. I played in a professional set-up. Then I loved living in Cork. I was very lucky, I had college friends down there as well. Most of those lads, they went on to have fairly good careers afterwards. Some better and some worse, but they all played for a long time. We were a good bunch of players.

When I went to Reading, I was doing the same training. I was probably fitter than most of them to be honest and probably stronger. It made it seamless for me. I was 21 years of age going to a club and I was not a kid going over. So, I had a lot of experience under my belt, even at 21... and big games in Ireland.

Through Cork City and playing well there, I got into the Ireland under-21 squad. It was a lot of development going on in those few years while I was at Cork City, personally. Still my argument with a lot of people remains... why would you go anywhere at 15 or 16, or look to go anywhere? Why wouldn't you stay? I know it is not for everyone and some lads are exceptionally talented maybe at 16, that it works for them to go to another club in another country.

But for me it was the perfect route. Cork City prepared me so well and it gave me a fabulous three years. I wasn't just there as a stepping stone. I was there to play and be a part of it for three years. My move to England came about because it went well. It was the ideal scenario.

I am actually disappointed at how Cork are now. I was looking at the League of Ireland Premier Division for 2022... and basically seeing every club is Dublin or north of Dublin. There is no club in the Premier Division south of the M50 basically.

I don't know what the story or situation is now, but I hope Cork City can get back. The League of Ireland needs Cork City because if they are doing well, it just makes the league having them there.

99

JOE GAMBLE

SHELBOURNE 0 ★ CORK CITY 2
League Of Ireland Premier Division
Tolka Park
MAY 30, 2005

Joe Gamble steers an inch perfect pass against St Pat's at Turner's Cross in 2008.

★ **SHELBOURNE:** S Williams; O Heary, J Harris , C Hawkins, D Rogers; B Ryan, S Byrne, J Crawford, J Ndo; J Byrne, G O'Neill. Subs: S Brennan for Rogers, W Hoolahan for Heary , G Crowe for J Byrne.

★ **CORK CITY:** M Devine; N Horgan, A Bennett, D Murray, B Woods; R O'Donovan, G O'Callaghan, C O'Brien, **J Gamble**; K Doyle, N Fenn. Subs: J O'Flynn for Doyle, G O'Halloran for O'Donovan , K Murray for Fenn.

THE ACTION

CORK CITY ROARED to the top of the League Of Ireland Premier Division table after a famous victory away to Shelbourne at Tolka Park.

This was very much a huge statement of intent for Damien Richardson's side to secure the three points away to their title rivals from Dublin.

Roy O'Donovan gave City the lead with a goal 10 minutes into the second-half. George O'Callaghan sprayed the ball out wide for Neale Fenn and when he picked out O'Donovan with a pinpoint cross, he headed astutely into the back of the net.

Shelbourne looked to pose questions of the visiting defence, but they found the City defence, including Dan Murray who was razor alert to deal with any danger. The home side commenced this game brightly, threatening to open the scoring on a number of occasions.

City doubled their advantage in the 74th minute. O'Callaghan and John O'Flynn combined well to put the Shelbourne defence under pressure, only for Shels' sub Stephen Brennan to knock a stabbed shot from the latter into his own net.

This was a victory built upon City's passing game and the quiet confidence that surrounded the Cork camp in the build-up to the fixture.

★★★★★

66

ONE HUNDRED PERCENT, Cork City FC was the most enjoyable spell of my playing career. It is not even close.

My affection for the club and the people who were there, that is a bond that I will never lose. Not necessarily just the club, but the people I shared this changing room with, the fellas who stood toe-to-toe together and the games we played together. They mean more to me than the club to be quite honest with you, because they are the people that you spend the time with and you spend the memories with. I am not playing that down to the people that were there at the club or the fans. The warm reception we used to get as players, the fans loved you. If you go around Cork, people know who you are and are asking about the game... the game last week and the game coming up.

It is only human nature, people love that. It is an affectionate thing that you always have, so I will be forever grateful for that. I will be forever grateful for the teammates that I played with and the memories that I have. There is no club after I left Cork City that I ever had the same connection with or the same grá for. My time with Cork City is only ever going to be fondly.

The Cork City dressing-room was the best by a long shot. I had good times at Limerick, there are great fellas up there I am still friendly with them. I was in Hartlepool, which was a different scenario where it was dog eat dog. They were nice people, but it was a job. When I was in Brunei, it was a totally different scenario abroad and lifestyle outside of football.

The craic I had with Cork City and the players, the shenanigans before and after training, mixing with the lads. It was actually like a proper dressing-room. There were no egos and no one thought that they were better than they were. It was just good lads who were the same age approximately, just living life and living the best life really and just getting on with it.

The one thing through all of that is when training came, it was serious. We were on that side of it as well where there was a seriousness and an edge to training.

That is why I think we were so good, we could divide that seriousness and our fun to work. That is the balance that we had without knowing it because they were the characters we had in the team. We had a fantastic team. I am not blowing anyone's trumpet, but if that team had stayed together for another two or three years, could we have won two or three titles on the bounce one hundred percent.

I think that it is one of the best teams that has played in the League Of Ireland. I have no doubt about it. The reason I am going to say that is because look at the players that were there and after that they have done or before what they have done.

Look at Kevin Doyle, who went on to play international football and had a fantastic career in the English Premiership. A top, *top* striker. Look at Roy O'Donovan, went onto play in the English Premier League with Sunderland, played in England and Australia for years. Alan Bennett was an Irish senior international.

I was lucky enough to play international and I was the first ever player to play for Ireland as a Cork City player. Neale Fenn an ex-Premier League centre-forward with Tottenham Hotspur. A magician, the best player I have ever played with a first touch. Dan Murray was probably the best centre-half ever to play for Cork City and doesn't get the recognition for it. But if you ask any player that played with him, an absolute top draw player. I am going to miss out on a load of players, I could name them all. We were blessed. So to win the league you have to have the calibre of player. That is why the league is so tough.

To win a league with Cork City was a big deal. To get over the line was a big deal. For me it was my first trophy I had ever won as a professional footballer. Some players go 15 to 20 years and not win a single thing. Some players can go four or five years and win four or five titles in-a-row. You just don't know. League titles, cups and silverware don't come every year. Some players might never ever get silverware. Some of the greatest players in the world might never win anything. So to win something and to win it with your hometown club, it's a huge deal. It is something that I will always cherish.

That stigma when you come back from England, that you've failed or whatever. I went to England and the four years I had at Reading shaped the rest of my football career. If I didn't go there, if I didn't get the education or the understanding of how to be a professional footballer… what it entails and how you need to live your life. All these sort of things, if I didn't go there is no way I'd have been living from the game for 17 years if I didn't get that apprenticeship.

That is the way I look at my time in England. I could have stayed in England as well, there were one or two offers. But I think at that time, mentality-wise, I just needed to come home.

Cork City were on the up and they were gone full time. So the timing was right. When you do come home, you want to prove your worth and want to prove that you are very good. You have to prove that you deserve to be at this level. Just who I am as a person as well. I always wanted to prove that I can cut it and I am a very good player in my own right, that I was never not going to succeed. That is not an arrogant thing, that was just a confidence thing within myself and who I am as a character. I always knew that I would be good enough to play and hopefully prove that I was one of the best midfielders that played for Cork City. That was my attitude and I needed to prove that.

The Derry game to win the league at Turner's Cross, I don't think I'll ever play a game that was as so important, so emotional and so intense, just built up for so long. I just think that it had everything. It was the last game of The Shed. Everyone associates Turner's Cross with the Shed and the atmosphere that was there. To win the game in the way it was done, we had to win that game as a draw wouldn't do.

I remember the build up to the game. People were looking for tickets three or four weeks in advance because they knew it was going to come down to that game. Just the rivalry that us and Derry had that year. The way we performed, the way we won the game itself and there was no doubt that we weren't going to win the game. It had everything and it was one of the greatest games I have ever been involved in. Even the games that might have more attraction to it like international football, nothing compared to beating Derry at Turner's Cross in the last game.

European games were special. When we played Slavia Prague at home, that was a good one. The Djurgårdens game at home for me was top notch. It was one of those where we were on level par with them in terms of standard and there wasn't much between the teams. We got a great draw away. But at home that was a great game and a great atmosphere. I think we were on the up that time.

Shelbourne were the top dogs and they were the best team in the country. They are the Dubs... Cork don't like Dublin and the Dubs don't like us. All of that incentive, it rolled into one. We came second the year before in 2004 and we were edging closer to winning the league. We went on a big unbeaten streak and when we played Shels in Tolka, we might have been threatening that success but we didn't have an awful lot of it. Shels were a brilliant team and had very good pros, older and more experienced and knew what it was to win the league. But we were just fearless.

We just went out there and said right... *we will stand toe-to-toe and we are going to beat ye.* That was the attitude that we had. We didn't look at them as this big great team that won so many leagues. We just looked at them equally and we went out there and we performed to win the game.

It just gave us that belief without saying it was the turning point, it just probably cemented that we are a very good team. I think that was a big game for us that year. Games against Shelbourne were big games. The game away really was a big one. But we really beat them and we were very good on the day. It gave us belief and that probably got us over the line to actually win the league, that game away. There was a big rivalry between us and Shels. We didn't like them and they didn't like us. We were the young pretenders and they were the older stalwarts of the league.

We were brash and we were confident. We just went up there and kicked them off the park, as well as played good football.

I just think, as a player, you want to go and win the game. You want to go and prove that you are better than your opponent. That is what it was. Most players don't' really see or hear what goes on in the crowd. At the end of the day it is a job and a professional job. There is an attachment obviously that you are from Cork and some lads would have supported Cork City. Ultimately, your head ruled your heart. You just go and win the game because you want to win every game, that is what it is.

We went into every game thinking we are going to win at home or away. We had very good players in key positions. We had excellent centre-halves and a strong midfield. We had excellent strikers and we were creative out wide, we had tough full-backs and an excellent goalkeeper. There was no real weak link in our team. You couldn't really say... *get after him, he is a weak player.*

We didn't have any weak links. We were just as good as one another. That is what sold us as a team, we just had good players. We could win the individual battles as well and we could win the team battles. So we had everything going.

I think as we were probably young and fearless, we just didn't realise the importance of some games. We were just going around feeling we are a good team. People might say we were bold or brash or arrogant. But we were just confident, and there is a difference between arrogance and confidence. We just knew to a man that on our day we'd beat you if we came up trumps. That was how I always perceived our team to be.

I was playing against Wes Hoolahan in the Shels side. I would have known Wes from underage international teams. He played left wing, right wing or he could also play in midfield. They had Joey Ndo in midfield. So there were good players

Shels also had the likes of Jim Crawford, Owen Heary... Jason Byrne. They were tough characters and they were men. They were not shrinking violets and they'd put it up to you. We just made sure we were giving as good as we got. They were big games. Every time we played them, I always probably played well. We played Shels another day on a Sunday afternoon at Turner's Cross and won 2-0.

We gave it to them, basically. Now again, there were games they would have given to us as well and we would have come out the other end of it. There was just a big rivalry there and they were just good games to play in.

A memory from the Shels game in Tolka Park, without doubt Roy O'Donovan calling out Owen Heary that time. Heary was a very good full-back then, but Roy put it up to him. Roy was only a young lad himself and I think was only 19 at the time. He was calling him out saying he wasn't good enough to play against Roy O'Donovan sort of a thing.

Roy did put it up to him and had an excellent game that day. I think that stood out to me, this bit of afters during the game, to say that... *we are not going to back down from ye... we are a serious team, we are going to put it up to ye.* I think Roy might have scored or crossed the ball for someone to score and there was a bit of verbals. But that happens in games. I think it is just passionate, it was just us kind of saying... *we are Cork City , we are here to play and we are here to win.*

MICHAEL DEVINE
(NEAL HORGAN, DAN MURRAY, ROY O'DONOVAN & JOHN O'FLYNN)

CORK CITY 2 ★ **DERRY CITY 0**
League Of Ireland Premier Division
Turner's Cross
NOVEMBER 18, 2005

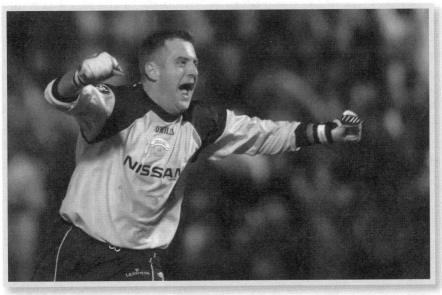

Michael Devine celebrates after teammate Liam Kearney scored Cork's second goal to clinch the 2005 league title against Derry City at Turner's Cross.

★ **CORK CITY: M Devine**; **N Horgan**, A Bennett, **D Murray**, D Murphy; **R O'Donovan**, G O'Callaghan, J Gamble, L Kearney; N Fenn, **J O'Flynn**. Subs: D Behan for Fenn, C O'Brien for O'Donovan, D Coughlan for O'Flynn.

★ **DERRY CITY:** D Forde; E McCallion, C Delaney, P Hutton, S Hargan; G McGlynn, C Martyn, K Deery , K Brennan; G Beckett, M Farren. Subs: P McCourt for Hargan, A Murphy for Deery, S O'Flynn for Martyn.

THE ACTION

CORK CITY WON the League Of Ireland Premier Division title for the first time since 1993 following a deserved home win against Derry City. In what was a final day title decider at a sold-out Turner's Cross, it was a contest which Damien Richardson's side not only won, but did so in style.

It was Cork City that struck for the opening goal of the contest on 18 minutes, when John O'Flynn headed in impressively beyond Derry 'keeper David Forde following a cross by Roy O'Donovan. City dominated the remainder of the half with some superb passing football, but it seemed as if the second goal may not arrive.

However, Cork did manage to hit the back of the net again just past the hour mark. Denis Behan did well to set up Liam Kearney, who rolled the ball past Forde in front of a packed Shed End to cement a famous night in the history of the club.

Derry City brought on Paddy McCourt and he was denied by a fine one handed save by Cork goalkeeper Michael Devine, who somehow kept out the Northern Ireland international's header from eight yards out, with Killian Brennan also going close for the away side.

But following a lengthy absence, the league title was at long last coming back to Leeside.

★★★★★

66

IT WAS SUCH a fabulous feeling, and it was such a fabulous night. I always wanted to win the league. I always wanted to win it because you knew that you were the best in the league that season. We fought all season for it, and we believed that we were the best team. Damien Richardson had us pumped up.

We just felt that we were going to win the title from the start of the season. That was just a magical night. I know it is hard to put it into words. I talk to my dad sometimes about it because he was there that night. After the game I was in his arms because I knew where he was sitting. He was delighted for me, and it was emotional and all that. I still get emotional now even thinking about it.

We knew we were going to go out and win it... we never doubted ourselves.

I remember from the last five or six games, the grounds were nearly full before the warm up. We used to go out early with the goalkeepers, an hour and 15 minutes beforehand and it would be three-quarters full. But that night against Derry, when we came out the place was hopping. It was just great and one of the best feelings in the world.

I am living in Cobh and was born in Cobh, but I would be a Cork City supporter. Just to win the league for your hometown club, and at home, with the place hopping... you couldn't write it... it was fairytale stuff.

All that Derry needed was a draw.

But there was no reason they were going to come down to Turner's Cross and play for a draw, not with Stephen Kenny as manager. I think just everybody wanted to be there because it was the last night of the Shed, and they knew we were going to win the league, it was as simple as that.

The City supporters were unreal. It was great for a goalkeeper like me to be around. If I did something well, they were cheering me on. It was like there was always somebody behind you to protect you and all that. I know sometimes they'd be shouting abuse at me, but that was a good thing... and it was only one or two.

I loved it, I really did love it ... the Shed. I know it is not the same these days, but I know there is fantastic support there. Everybody knows that the Shed was magical.

I think I was always the same really in terms of my preparation. Personally, I was always just looking forward to games because I hated training. I know there is a new stand there now, but the Shed was just special. Even for the opposition 'keepers, it gave then some craic.

If an opposing 'keeper took it honestly and took it well, the Shed would have a laugh with him. Stephen O'Brien of Longford Town, I remember when we were playing Longford at home and the Shed would be onto Stephen, but Stephen would give it back. The City fans loved it and it was only good banter. It was just a magical place.

Phil Harrington, the legend of Cork City was there and he was our goalkeeping coach. He'd never let you rest on your laurels because Phil has been through it and done the lot. Myself and Nults (Mark McNulty) got on really well and we still do to be fair. He's been a legend for the club over the years.

With Phil, you would have a great warm up before a game. He always had you mentally prepared; it doesn't matter if you were playing bad or good, you'd still be the same. He would know things. He'd just talk to you and calm you down. Sometimes, you'd be a bit excited and he'd see in the warm up that you were being a little bit hesitant. He'd talk to you and calm you down just to take it easy. He was great to have. Everybody respected him... even the outfield players when he spoke.

I really enjoyed playing, and keeping a clean sheet was even better. Neal Horgan, Alan Bennett, Dan Murray, Danny Murphy... they were so good. Dan only came in a couple of years and was the captain. Everybody looked up to him. Dan was a good few years younger than me. But I still looked up to him because when Dan did speak, you'd listen to his kind of way... he knew his stuff.

Alan Bennett was just a trojan, he was just a giant sometimes on the pitch. Danny Murphy, the Cockney Rebel, what could you say about him? Danny could take the biggest player on the pitch and wouldn't care... no bother to him. Neal was just a gentleman. He was very underrated as a player. He was very good, and there were never many fellas who would beat him in terms of pace or beat him in the air. He never got the recognition he deserved nationally. He did from Cork City and the fans. From the League of Ireland, I think he should have been called up a few times, called into squads or under-21s or something like that.

George O'Callaghan was absolutely brilliant. John O'Flynn... he was born to score goals. Kevin Doyle had eight or nine goals at the start of that season.

We had super players. Roy O'Donovan was like lightning. Roy is still playing at the top level in Australia and he is winning awards left, right and centre. Liam Kearney, Denis Behan... the team we had was spectacular.

Everybody just contributed throughout the whole season and it was great.

When Damien Richardson came in, we just did football... *football, football* every single day. Damien would talk to you about problems and all that, he was very good. I got on well with him before, when I was at Cobh Ramblers at the start... he came in to Cobh as manager there. So, I knew him personally that kind of way and I got on well with him. Damien helped my game a lot.

I think we had an FAI Cup final two or three weeks later, so we couldn't relax and enjoy it that much, but a few of us still did. It was a sense of relief, I knew we were going to win the game, but still the feeling that we had won it and done it, it was just absolutely magical.

We all went back to the Rochestown Park Hotel that night for a few drinks. Even the Derry lads were back there; they were staying that night. It was a great night in there, that is all I'll say. Just to celebrate with the fans and to win the league at home! I was in the Shed at one stage after the game, with boots, gloves and everything.

I think we were always in control of the game. They only had one chance in the whole game. We had a few chances. To be fair, there were a lot of good players on the pitch for Derry City as well. I'd say it was a good game of football. I have watched the game back now a few times afterwards, and it is still a good game to watch.

Some of the games you watch in the League of Ireland over the last couple of years can be dour sometimes. But to have a league decider, everything on the line that night, it must have been a great game of football to watch and especially if you were a Cork City fan. Then we met some of the Derry City fans afterwards... Derry and Cork City always have a bit of a special bond, really.

I won Player of the Year with Cork City, so I was happy with that. I got Goalkeeper of the Year as well with the Soccer Writers of Ireland. So, I was very happy. To get Player of the Year, that season, especially with the likes of Georgie and John O'Flynn... all the boys getting all the goals. I was surprised, but delighted.

Cork City would have been the most enjoyable spell of my playing career.

It was fantastic to be there and I always wanted to be there. Even when I was down in Waterford, I just wanted to be at Cork. At the time Liam Murphy got onto me and Derek Mountfield signed me. So, I was really delighted.

I hope that the fans still think of me well up there. I think they do, every time I've been there I have always felt appreciated.

NEAL HORGAN

Neal Horgan (centre top) celebrates with teammates Danny Murphy, Derek Coughlan, Greg O'Halloran and Alan Bennett, after victory against Shelbourne in the league in 2005.

"

FOR ME, IT was about winning leagues, winning cups, being at the very pinnacle of the game in Ireland. The 2005 game was amazing in that it put all of that on the line in one match. That we could be heroes or people who didn't quite get there.

The fact that Derry were ahead of us meant we had to win. Whilst anyone coming to the game that day would have known that, they might not have known Neal Horgan had been trying to achieve this his entire life.

This might be the closest we'd ever get to achieving what we were trying to achieve! It was all going to be decided in 90 minutes in front of 8,000 to 10,000 screaming people tightly packed into Turner's Cross. It really set it up to be a really important game. I knew, and all the rest of the players knew, this was going to have an impact on the rest of our lives, as to how we maybe look back at our careers… were we right to stick with football or not?

It is very important to mention Derek Coughlan, who was a huge influence when we were walking out at the start of the game. He started shouting 'We are in Cork… we are going to win and nobody is going to take it from us'.

That really got us all in the right place, as did Damien Richardson and Dave Hill, who did really good jobs that day as well.

Damien made a big impression in the dressing-room, playing it low key, telling us 'To trust ourselves'. That was the right kind of chord for me.

Dave Hill actually gave me advice as we were in the warm up. The thing about that game was, we turned up at the Turner's Cross Tavern as we normally would maybe two and a half hours before the game… and it was full of Derry fans.

Normally, it was just us in there.

So, this was different to the normal prep for a game. Now, we had anticipated this to some degree, but it can be a bit disturbing. Then you go out to do the warm up. Again, this is an hour and a half before the game. Normally there was a few fans, but on this night the ground was full.

Everyone who was going to the game was at the match. The ground was full and you are like *F**k this is different*. Normally you have a chance to wind up… normally, you go from a situation where it is just you in dressing-room and then you get to go out onto the pitch and see a few fans. You are getting ready… the music is starting. Normally, you go back into the dressing-room and you hear the crowd coming in and you hear the chants starting up.

The Derry game in 2005 was different.

The crowd were there before we were there. The getting ready or jazzing up is done. Luckily, Dave Hill called me aside and said 'Do you know what you do on nights like this? You just breathe in the air,'… as in breathe in the crowd.

'Have a look straight at them, breathe it in and just take it from there.' So, you got the crowd through your system, somehow by breathing them in. And that helped.

The very first incident I was involved in was a kick out from the Derry goalkeeper over to my side. By hell, I was going to win this header… the Derry player could have been 10 feet tall, it didn't matter… I was going to jump and I was going to win this ball.

I won the header, which was great. I had Roy O'Donovan primed as well. That was a great start for me… you're in the game and I got a bit of a roar. It was something that probably boosted me. You needed to meet the game, be there and be ready. So, I was ready and that header helped.

John O'Flynn scored a great goal, Roy O'Donovan crossing it in for him… and Liam Kearney got a great finish after Denis crossed it for him. About 10 minutes to go and you can imagine now… 2-0 is the worst lead in football, as they say. It is definitely not a statistically correct comment. But they say the worst lead in football is 2-0 because if they get one, the momentum goes the other way and you could end up going backwards.

Derry launched a counter-attack. From the middle of the pitch, I spotted Ciarán Martyn, the Derry attacking midfielder, and a guy that I knew was originally from Sligo. What he was brilliant at was scoring goals from midfield. I'd say he has more goals from midfield in that era than any other midfielder. I was well aware of Ciarán from years before.

I had played against him in an All-Ireland final with my school Coláiste An Spioraid Naoimh back in 1998. Spioraid Naoimh have a very good soccer tradition. They are strong in other sports too. Brian Barry-Murphy would have played soccer there as well actually, and a few others. But John Egan is probably the outstanding example.

Anyway, we had gone and lost two All-Irelands in 1996 and '98 both in the final, and both away from home. So, I had lost those on the last day of the season. The 1996 final was in Terryland Park against St Mary's of Galway. There was a guy called Darragh Sheridan who subsequently went on to Villa… he scored two goals in the last minute pretty much. We had been winning 1-0.

Two years later, the same group of players get to the final and we played Summerhill Sligo in McSharry Park, which was in Sligo, which was just the way it was. We lost to Sligo after extra-time, 3-2. That kind of stuff… for me I needed to get over those defeats and they were heart-breaking defeats. Particularly, I felt I didn't play to my best in those games.

If we had won the 1996 game, we would have been going to a European Championships effectively for schools. So that St Mary's Galway team went to play in Cyprus or Greece, and we were distraught by this. As I said, we'd been winning 1-0 with six minutes to go.

Then in 1998 against Summerhill Sligo, we were hoping to slay that dragon. But they had a very good team. Conor O'Grady, whom I later played with at City, was in midfield… and they had a few other future League of Ireland players, including a guy named Flanagan who scored an unbelievable overhead kick in the final.

They also, as I said, had Ciarán Martyn, who, I think scored in the game too. It was the last time a lot of us would play together. Two of our best players, Kevin O'Riordan (Skippy) and James O'Sullivan have sadly parted from us since then. For whatever reason, we never quite conquered that Irish summit together, but we came very close and won Munster titles with club and school on four or five occasions.

So, I was well aware in 2005 of the existence and threat of Ciarán Martyn in Derry's midfield. Now, cut to City being 2-0 up… looking to hang on for the glorious and long-awaited league title. There must have been about 10 minutes left.

Derry broke down the pitch… their right winger had the ball and he is crossing it from deep into the box. Ciarán Martyn is running towards our penalty box.

He has got on the other side of Joe Gamble.

Joe starts shouting 'Hoggy… Hoggy…' essentially meaning get across to cover Martyn, and I come across from my side. I don't need to be asked twice.

He, of all people, is not going to score tonight.

Just as that happens, it is crossed in, comes back out again… and I am still with Ciarán Martyn. It is crossed to the back post and Paddy McCourt is there. He heads the ball and Devine makes a brilliant save. Luckily for me Devine does so, because I'd have been blamed I'd say for Derry getting back into the match.

What I wasn't allowing to happen, come rain or shine, was Ciarán Martyn score because of a scar I had from Sligo back in 1998. He was not scoring in Turner's Cross.

That brings you to what it is, it is a personal journey that we all take. The Derry guys, including their manager at the time Stephen Kenny went on to have great careers afterwards. But all of those guys with the Cork City team, they all got there through different routes. I think that game in particular, because it gave us a league win and we came through different routes… it has a different value for all of us.

My thoughts at full time? Sheer relief, I suppose, because if you are a defender, this could go from absolute joy to unfathomable tragedy in the blink of an eye, and you could be the culprit. That is in your head for the game, but the last 10 minutes in particular. You need to be on top of this and make sure everything is as it is, defensively.

So, you are carrying that the entire season, but in particular in this game. You could be massively exposed here to something that is beyond you. You are kind of protective a bit, but you have to carry the burden and you have to act.

When the whistle blows then, you are released from that burden and it's gone well. You are just in *La La Land*. Figuratively, like someone pulls back a big string like, elastic… you had been held back, but suddenly you are flown forward.

We were jettisoned into the Shed, which was great. It was just amazing.

We had family on the pitch, friends on the pitch. It was absolutely fabulous because it was warranted. The club hadn't won a league title in 12 years, and everyone knew what it meant. It was a real statement or stamp!

When you look at that 2005 team, I'd say each and every one of them, apart from me, had been to England and come back. Maybe Alan Bennett hadn't, but did subsequently. In your head you have all these kinds of things that are personal to you and you'd think maybe… *I am not up to this level.*

But actually, now you had the medal!

The demons were gone! You actually had the medal to show those demons were wrong. *You are up to this level and you have won the league.* For me, it was the pinnacle of everything that I wanted to do in football. Obviously, everyone wants to play with Ireland or play cross channel or in Europe if you could, and that didn't happen for me.

But winning a league with Cork City? That was always on the bucket list. I'm so glad we achieved it.

In respect to that game, the Shed was gone after that night. It was a magnificent day for the club. I think it should have sent signals out to people above us in the League of Ireland and in the FAI, that we are sitting on something here that could explode in terms of popularity.

At the time it was an amazing product, and we had about six full-time clubs. I know people go back to sustainability and all that, but the FAI did nothing to help full-time clubs after that point. Which for me is galling, and I have written books afterwards and they all have been primarily motivated by the lack of support for the League of Ireland.

Anyone who was at that game, remembers it. You still have guys come up to you and say 'I was at that game that day!' For us, it was that important... it was like our Cork City v Bayern Munich game. The game my generation are most asked about.

It is unfortunate we didn't keep that squad for longer, for various reasons. But that team could have been the foundation of a side who really achieved in Europe. We were close, but we could have really achieved something. I mean, not through the champions backdoor route... I think we could have gotten to where Shelbourne got at the time in Europe and further, if we had improved upon that group.

What we had though was Mick Devine, who was an outstanding goalkeeper, and we had Mark McNulty on the bench. It should be noted that Phil Harrington, who must have been around 41 at the time... for about three games that year, Phil played in goals and got clean sheets. That was unreal.

Mick got injured over in Lithuania. I actually collided with him and he got injured from a cross. He jumped into my knee is how I will explain it!

Anyway, he was injured for three games as a result. Now Mark McNulty was already out... he'd pulled his hamstring. And so Phil Harrington, our goalkeeper coach was put on the bench because Mark was out.

Next thing Phil is playing. Myself and Danny Murphy took the kickouts, because Phil couldn't take the kickouts with his legs. 'My legs are f***ed,' he'd tell us in his strong Welsh accent. He kept three clean sheets in Europe and in the league, and in particular a hugely important clean sheet against Drogheda, who beat us in the cup final later.

We had a very good back four, but actually we had a great back eight or nine. We had eight or nine great defenders in the squad who could be called upon at any time. As a defensive four, you want the same guys there all of the time if you can. Luckily for me, I played every game that year. What we had in reserve, and this is what wins you things, was Derek Coughlan at centre-back who has won numerous leagues and cups, Greg O'Halloran who could play anywhere, Cillian Lordon who could play anywhere like Greg, Colin O'Brien who was massively experienced and also could fit in at right full. We also had Kevin Murray who was outstanding on his day and was later captain of Cobh.

That is five proper players, on top of the back four that we had. So, we knew if we slipped up, those guys would come in and take our place. Thankfully, as a back four we gelled and we got results.

Damien Richardson wasn't the kind of guy that changed things, if they were going well. Damien gave you that kind of trust, I think.

In midfield obviously Joe Gamble and George O'Callaghan were outstanding. They were brilliant players on their own, but they played a separate kind of role to each other. They weren't two midfielders who played together… Joe would defend and attack aggressively on his own. He was tigerish in defence, and tigerish in attack. George was spectacularly skilful. I played with him in the Kennedy Cup, so I would have known George a long time before he went over to Port Vale and came back. It was a nice thing for me and him to win it together too.

On the wings, Roy O'Donovan would have come in that season. He just fit in and was like the missing piece of the jigsaw in many ways. Liam Kearney was a very smart player, very fit, with a full-time ethos and could score goals in important games.

Colin O'Brien played loads of games that season… Greg O'Halloran played loads of games that season in the middle of the park. Cillian Lordan played right wing plenty of times. Billy Woods played a hell of a lot of games… and Billy could have played that day, because he did very well leading up to it.

That was the one decision I think Rico had to make coming into that game, was whether to start Billy or Liam Kearney. He decided on Liam, which worked in the end. Up front we had the selection of selections. At the start of the year, we had Kevin Doyle, Roy O'Donovan, Neale Fenn, John O'Flynn, George O'Callaghan and Denis Behan. So that was the kind of group that we had. And the guys trying to break into that group like Shane Long, Cathal Lordan and Admir Softic were outstanding players as well.

I actually think, looking back, we've never had a stronger group in my period at the club. When we lost Doyler and Shane Long… particularly Doyler because Shane Long was developing, but you could already see the athleticism Shane had was unbelievable.

Kevin Doyle was a big part of that team. Afterwards I went over to Kevin in England. I'd have a good relationship with him, and at the time he was living near me. We were both living in rented accommodation near UCC. Kevin used to pick me up and we'd go to training. At the time, we trained in Deerpark school. We used to go to training and we'd pick up Admir Softic along the way as well. I felt that Kevin had a huge part in the winning of that league, because he had scored a lot of goals that year and had played I'd say 11 or 12 league games. So, I went over after we won the league… he got me tickets, which was very nice of him, and me and my friends went over to the Madejski Stadium.

The *Examiner* had given us all a very nice thing, it was a framed version of the front page of their paper the day after we won the league because we made the front page. So I brought that over to Kevin and I think he was happy with it.

If we had that group of players for the next two or three years, and we added one or two players, honestly, we could have broken all kinds of glass ceilings. We were moving in one direction only. We had the talent, the momentum… and we had the crowd.

Unfortunately, after that game in 2005, it never reached that height again. I know we won the Setanta Cup and the FAI Cup. But we were never as good as we were then. But in a way, it was the right place to reach your peak. It was the right game. If we had lost that and won the cup final two weeks after, it wouldn't have been as good. It wouldn't have been as momentous. It was unfortunate we lost the cup final, but that's another day's work.

It was the peak and is possibly the best group of players Cork City FC have ever had, that is possibly… and I am biased. The squad was put together by Liam Murphy, Pat Dolan and finally by Damien Richardson, all under the supervision of Brian Lennox who was, of course, chairman. But if you think of the squad, it was unreal.

In fairness to the 1992/1993 team, they wouldn't have had a big of squad because of the nature of football at that time. Also, they were part-time whereas we were full-time and that is different too. So maybe it is unfair to compare them in terms of a squad. Their first 11 or 13 players were really top players… heroes of mine to this day. City also had an outstanding side in 1998/99 that were very unlucky not to win a league title, or even two.

I do think we had a better squad than John Caulfield's 2017 double-winning squad. They had some great players too and a fantastic front three, but I think overall we were stronger. I just think that's a high watermark for full-time football at Cork City. That high watermark was reached that day against Derry because we performed excellently.

That was the beauty of it as well... after all that pressure, everything going into it and all those things happening, that we played really well and dominated. It is a lovely thing to be able to look back on... a *lovely* thing.

The 2005 League of Ireland title-winning game is life changing. I played GAA as well but the level I reached playing that day with Cork City is something I am very proud of. I think the fact I was from Cork makes winning the league for your home club very, *very* special, particularly in what is a Dublin dominated league.

Dundalk were an anomaly in that sense, though they had a lot of Dublin-based players. At the time we won the league, we had three lads from England... Danny Murphy, Dan Murray and Neale Fenn.

It was lovely to have the lads from England and we needed them. Like, we were primarily Cork guys and it was nice because none of us intended to live anywhere else for the rest of our lives. Every one of us, I think, wanted to go and play in England for the next 10 years if we could and then come back to Cork.

The league title was always going to be there for us when we lived in Cork, something we could share with people. I still do, to this day. It is a lovely thing and I am glad that I have it. I don't know what it would be like if I didn't have it.

It was like an icing on the cake, that I can say we won that league title.

DAN MURRAY

Cork City captain Dan Murray celebrates with teammates after lifting the League of Ireland trophy in 2005.

❝

THE CELEBRATIONS AFTER the game, you never forget... being part of, and being in the middle of it. Lifting the trophy in Turner's Cross is pretty special, whatever trophy it is really.

It was my first major trophy as a player and as a captain. That is what you are judged on or that it was I judged myself on... what you win and how you do it.

It will always bring a smile to my face. The group of people that were in that team, I'd still be speaking to... the togetherness that team had was as important as winning the trophy. But it was a good time... fond memories. It was the highlight of my Cork City career, for sure.

At the time for Cork City, we had the best team and the best players. I think everything came together for us to win the league.

We were in a good place. Pat Dolan had us for a couple of years and then he left. Damien Richardson came in at the start of the 2005 season. We had an unbelievable belief that this was our year to win the league. When you look at it, it felt right that we had to win that match and to be in Turner's Cross was as good as it can get really.

We played well on the night… everyone was buzzing for it. And the city was fully behind the club.

At the time, it was probably the biggest sporting event that weekend in Cork and that probably doesn't happen that much with Cork City in the last few years. But everyone was behind us and everyone was keen to get a ticket for the game, which doesn't happen all of the time. We probably could have got over 10,000 people in, if you got everyone who wanted to be there into Turner's Cross.

That was my first trophy as a professional player.

So that made it even more special. That team was a pretty tight group and everyone was mainly from Cork…. it was a good squad to be involved in. We felt it was our year, if we wanted to go and get it really. We were winning game after game, and very rarely were losing.

We got to the cup final that year as well. The momentum just kept us going, and *going*. The place was pretty much full by the time we were warming up… so the buzz around the place, and the buzz during the warm up was really good. You could hardly hear what anyone was saying.

We were ready for it and in the dressing-room, Derek Coughlan closed the door, calmed everyone down and said 'lads… no excuses, let's go!' He was a big personality in the squad, he was a big player and his experience in the league was unreal. If he spoke everyone listened. That was part of it, and there was no ego from anyone in the squad. If someone had something to say, you listened. Derek had won titles; he won the title up in Bohs a couple of years before. So, he knew what it was all about, and we were always going to listen to him every time he ever spoke.

Fenny (Neale Fenn) had to go off early enough with a hamstring injury, I think it was. I remember Denis Behan came on and it was one of his best games that he had. I thought we were the better team on the night. I can't remember them really having a chance. When John O'Flynn scored the first goal that settled us down completely. Then we were comfortable throughout the game.

We probably could have won by more. The goal in front of the Shed to make it more comfortable… I can remember the noise for sure after that went in. Everyone remembers the trophy going into the Shed and stuff like that, which you probably wouldn't be allowed to do now.

When I first came over to Cork, there were a few full-time players, but mostly part-time players or people who worked that were training with us. It was strange to get my head around that you'd be training in the morning with six or seven players, and in the evening you'd be going to train with the rest of the squad. John O'Flynn was in England where I was, so I knew him already. That made it easier coming over and all I wanted to do was play football, enjoy my football, because I wasn't getting that many games in England.

You have to buy into what Cork is like. If you buy into it, you see the better players like Steven Beattie and Danny Murphy, the sort of players who have come down to Cork and have done well. Players who have come from outside and brought into Cork, they love Cork and they are the most successful players. That is what I say if anyone asks me if they are ever coming to Cork, just buy into Cork and enjoy Cork.

That is what I did. I came over and enjoyed it. I never thought I'd be staying for as long as I have stayed.

There was a core of really good lads of a similar sort of age; it was a great sort of atmosphere for me to come into. The club was probably slightly behind the Shels and the Bohs that year I joined.

The club was trying to turn… Brian Lennox was trying to turn the club to win the league. So, it was good to be a part of it. You could see it getting better and better each season when I came in… and 2005 was when it all came together perfectly. The rewards for what people put into the club came to fruit, really.

By the time we got to that last game of the season, there weren't many nerves in the changing room. It was just enthusiasm and hunger to go and win it, to win another football match… to win a league. There were some seriously good players that weren't starting every week. Shane Long was only just coming through as a young lad, but some weeks he wouldn't get on the bench because we had such a strong bench of players that were fully League of Ireland players. It was strong. Training was of a real high standard.

If you didn't train, you almost knew you weren't going to play. If you weren't going to play, you knew there was a player who could take your place. So very rarely did players miss training. There were four days a week everybody would be training and there would be no one sitting out, because they knew they weren't going to play the game that weekend. If they didn't play, they weren't going to get in the team, which I always feel breeds success in a team. You are not going to play unless you train, and train well. I think that showed that season. From training to matches, there wasn't too much of a let-down in the tempo and the standard because everyone knew what was expected of them.

For me, Damien Richardson had total confidence in the players. He let a lot of players be as good as they can be. He was honest with the players and he gave us the freedom just to go and win matches. He had full belief in us as players and we fed off that… that he had the belief. No matter what, he'd back you all of the way.

I think those years there from 2004 up to '09, it was brilliant and I loved it. I loved living in Cork and I loved playing for Cork City. It was my dream job to be a professional footballer and I was having the time of my life, really. I won a couple of leagues up at Shamrock Rovers and loved playing up there, but I will always say Cork City was a special time for me to be involved in the club and I felt a massive part of the city and the club for a good few years.

The partnership I had with Benno (Alan Bennett) was really, *really* good. We knew each other really well… strengths, weaknesses, who was better at what and stuff like that. It was just a build-up of years that we had been playing together. It was a top partnership.

That goes for the back four… Hoggy and Danny Murphy, and the goalkeeper Mick Devine. We played pretty much ninety-five percent of the games that season. We had the best defensive record, and that only comes from being able to play together and working on stuff like that.

We believed that we were never going to concede goals, which was our *goal*. We didn't really talk about it during the season because we were winning matches. But that is where we were at, really. Myself and Benno were of a similar age. We knew where we were at and what we wanted to do. The partnership was just getting to its best them two years in 2005 and '06.

If you look back on any team that wins a league, then they are normally not far off, if not the best defensive record in the division. It is no secret, if you don't concede goals then you have got a good chance of winning matches. We knew that and we knew the players that we had going forward, that we were always going to create chances and score goals. We didn't scream from the rooftops to say that we were the best at this or defending this. But we went into every match expecting to keep a clean sheet between the four or five of us.

Whoever was playing in goal or the back four, we knew if we kept a clean sheet, more than likely we would win matches. I think Mick and that back four, we judged ourselves on clean sheets more than anything else.

Being part of Cork City history is really good and it was the time of your life, really. I was young enough to enjoy everything, other stuff more than I should have done, but it was a really good time and I loved playing for Cork City.

You think it is going to happen more often than it does. Three Premier Division titles, however, is probably not enough for how big Cork is. It means so much to people in Cork, and Cork people always get behind winning teams and follow them till the end.

When Cork City are doing well in the league or in the cup, it is the talk of the town and there is a bit more buzz in the city than say a normal week. Probably my best moment in a Cork City jersey was that night. It always brings good memories back.

When I stopped playing a few years back, I still missed the playing part of it, but you get too old and it is harder to do when you are working. I have really enjoyed the coaching part of it a lot more than I thought I was probably going to. I have been lucky to work with the players I have worked with in the Cork City academy the last few years with the under-15s, under-17s and under-19s. It has been really good.

There is a really good set of players and a good group of coaches within the academy to work with. Colin Healy and Liam Kearney, they are putting everything in place, which is really exciting for the future. The pathway there for the players now is there for all to see.

ROY O'DONOVAN

Roy O'Donovan blasts home for Cork in the 2005 season.

"

HONESTLY, IT WAS very special.

It was my first year as a first team player. I had come back from England as an 18-year-old disillusioned with why haven't I made it cross channel? I got an opportunity to play for my hometown team, so it meant a hell of a lot to me to play with Cork City, in front of my family and my friends.

For that whole year, the way that it went… I got a go in the team, and I played quite well. Turner's Cross was bouncing, I can still feel the energy now. It makes the hairs on the back of the neck stand up. It was an unbelievably special game and moment in my career. It was just a truly terrific end to what was a wonderful year in Cork City's history.

Leading into the game that week, I just always felt a positive energy within the group. I genuinely say this, and I don't say this for a soundbite, I didn't sense any doubt in our mind that at Turner's Cross we weren't going to get the job done. It was just an air of invincibility and positivity about us that week. I would find it hard to pinpoint why, but we just had that confidence. It was a buzz leading up to that game for a couple of weeks in Cork. The crowds were building, and the excitement was getting bigger.

Personally, I felt really good in the game. I felt very fit, and I felt very strong. I was full of confidence at the time. When we opened the scoring, I put a cross in for John O'Flynn. As soon as it left my foot and the area that it was in, there was only going to be one outcome. When Flynny wheeled off to celebrate, that was the sense of relief that I think we needed to kick on again.

I think after we scored that first goal, we played some very fluid football. We passed the ball really well and played an attacking style that everybody enjoyed right throughout the league watching.

After the game, I just never forget the emotion. As a manager it was Damien Richardson's first League of Ireland title. He is someone that had an attachment to the league for 40 years, with his own father being a coach of St Pat's, as well. For him to win his first league trophy for Cork City was special for him and it was special for us. But I always just remember Derek Coughlan being lifted on people's shoulders.

We were all standing on the wall facing the old Shed. You just don't get moments like that anymore and probably will never get a moment like that again. It is very hard to appreciate how special it was.

Within the game, my own performance… I just remember every time I got the ball, I could feel a sense of excitement from the crowd. I tried to play my game with a bit of freedom as a winger. I was making a lot of mazy runs. I was unlucky not to score, but I was creating chances.

I set up the first goal and I had a part in the second goal that Liam Kearney scored. There were a few moments in the game that, really, I felt just untouchable. In my career, there have been a few times where things have happened in a game that I didn't realise or remember until I watched the footage back later.

Maybe that's the definition of being in *the zone*… when you read books and hear athletes being in the zone. There are certain times of your career when you get into it and I was definitely in the zone that night.

I had my balloon popped a little bit leaving England. I still thought that I had plenty to offer, and my talent wasn't utilised enough and all that. The best thing that ever happened in my career was the opportunity to represent Cork City.

I was a fan growing up and I got to play for Cork City at a time when it was a special time to be involved. It was a special group and the success that we had in the space of 12 months, it changed my outlook and my life. I will be forever grateful for it.

Cork City was my grounding. I think that you can learn all you want in the youth teams, and you can learn all you want in underage football, but ultimately men's football is different and that is why only 0.001% of people go on to make a game of it in the men's game. It is different to kids' football… it is completely different to the academy.

You learn to toughen up quick, and it is sink or swim.

Cork City taught me how to swim. Playing with vocal, confident men… tough guys, great players and great teammates. I got a few slaps along the way but, ultimately, they taught me how to be a first team player and how to be a leader. That year has certainly propelled my career onto where I am now. Nearly 20 years down the line in a professional career and I still reflect on my days at Cork City as some of the best that I have ever had.

I am truly blessed to have called it home.

To play in a first team in front of big crowds… and we were getting big crowds then! To have that expectation grow all the time. From when I got in the team, people expected more and more from me all the time. Not just my teammates, but the supporters. To be able to play and handle that kind of pressure and scrutiny and keep improving, that is only something you can learn on the job. You can only learn if you are able for it in that moment.

I felt at times at Cork City, in that first year especially, I had a lot of learning moments where I had to get back to basics. I had to go back to basics to find what was it that makes me a good player. You forget the basic things at times, and you start complicating the game.

I went home to my dad one day after I was going through a difficult two or three game period, and he said to me 'listen, get back to basics, just make your runs and try to score your goals… try to put the ball into the box and create chances for other people'. Pat Morley, a club legend, said the same thing to me one time when I hadn't scored a goal in three or four games, a bit of a drought for me at the time.

'It's very simple Roy, you just keep getting in there!' Pat told me. Meaning, keep getting in the box. Those kinds of moments, them tough times is what makes you appreciate the good times and I had plenty of good times.

I have spoken about a game that I didn't even score in. But I went on to score 40 odd goals in 100 games for Cork City. So, I learnt a hell of a lot and it was just a magical time to be a Cork City player.

For me, Damien Richardson was one of the best. It was one of the most enjoyable periods of my career working for Damien. I thought, first and foremost, he was a top-quality human being. He was just a great person, well able to talk to people. He was a really good man-manager. A lot of people come into management now with an arrogance of having their coaching badges and they want to play a certain style of football. I feel that they forget that they were once footballers themselves. It is difficult to get out there every week and to perform at the highest level and highest standards.

To get the best out of people, you need to know how to manage different qualities in different people. Damien was a master at that. I think he was obviously an older man at the time, but that experience as a human being, it just made a better coach. He let us as a team express ourselves... our attacking qualities, and he let us be ourselves. He reaped the benefits of that, really. We reaped the benefits of that in getting the chance to work with someone like him.

I always say that I was very blessed to play with that group, me as the young kid at the time. If you are looking at me now, with a beard... I am the older senior statesman and I am still playing now. Then being the upstart and the young kid coming through, I was very blessed to work with the people that I was surrounded by.

You are talking about the likes of Kevin Doyle and Shane Long who went onto do great things. But within that side, there really were five or six that could have gone on to play at higher levels or got caps. It was just probably a little bit of bad luck or bad timing on their part it didn't go that way.

But maybe they remember Cork City as being some of their finest days.

Going right through that team... Mick Devine in goal was the best of his era in the League of Ireland. You had Dan Murray and Alan Bennett, who dovetailed brilliantly, Dan Murray being the football player and Alan Bennett being the athlete that had pace to cover. Danny Murphy and Hoggy (Neal Horgan)… unbelievable, sensible and solid full-backs. He did a lot of defending for me… poor Hoggy.

Liam Kearney was a great winger, a cult hero in Cork. He took on some of the biggest and baddest defenders in the League of Ireland, and Joe Gamble who took one some of the biggest and baddest midfielders in the League of Ireland. For two lads that were only five feet tall standing on a chair, that's saying something!

Georgie, again another cult hero in Cork and who on his day was magic. John O'Flynn when he was fit, there were not many better goalscorers around. He was a terrific foil for somebody like me, who made runs and liked to put the ball into areas for a striker to be on the end of it. Neale Fenn was one of my favourite strike partners when I played at Cork City. He wasn't the quickest player, but up in his head he was two steps ahead and he was a great foil for me when I eventually moved up to being a striker.

That is just the starting team. You are talking about Derek Coughlan, Billy Woods and Colin O'Brien from the old stock in the squad… Denis Behan and Greg O'Halloran. Honestly, we had a bit of everything in that team. I look back now with a lot of joy.

I remember there was a few of us that went into the dressing-room after the game, thinking they'd set up before we come back out to lift the cup. Then, nobody came in. We went back out and Dan Murray, by that time… he was lifting the cup. I made a quick dart to jump on someone's back, it might have even been Noelle Feeney, God rest her… just to get in amongst the celebrations!!

I always remember going back to Rochestown Park afterwards. I didn't drink as I wanted to savour it and I wanted to take it all in. Of all the places that I have played and all of the players that I have played with, there is still a group of us that are friends. They say there are no friends it football… well, that team certainly bucked that trend because we're all very close. When we get the chance to catch up and have a beer, it is great. We don't do it often enough, as obviously a lot of us live in various locations. But we are not far away from a 20-year reunion.

I have had various times in my career. The last six years in Australia have been very enjoyable. A great challenge and a great standard of football. The life-balance in Australia… with the sunshine. I am one of the all-time top scorers in the A League here, as well. It is a part of my career in my thirties that I have had a bit of a resurgence as such. Playing in the Premier League at Sunderland under Roy Keane was another special time in my career. I got to play against the best in the business. I represented Ireland at various times in my life, and it was always very special to hear the national anthem play.

But Cork City is a time in my career I hold very dear. It holds a very important part in my foundations as a football player. Unfortunately, I didn't get a chance to play for Cork City for a longer period.

But you never know, I mightn't have put on the shirt for the last time.

JOHN O'FLYNN

John O'Flynn beats Derry City goalkeeper David Forde to score his side's first goal in the deciding game of the 2005 season and (inset) chases Liam Kearney after Cork's second goal.

"

FROM AN ALL-ROUND perspective, the 2005 title decider can't be beaten. Personally, for me, leading into the last game of 2005 against Derry, we knew it was going to be the last night of the Shed at Turner's Cross. So, it was a historical event. It is definitely my favourite game and when any anniversary of that game comes up on something like social media, it always gets fans talking... and memories build up again and it comes back to you.

I think maybe three or four weeks before the Derry game, I picked up a groin injury and it was down to the Wednesday before the game that I got the all-clear to be involved... at a capacity where my strength and conditioning coach was saying 'if you have a chance where you are going to smash the ball, don't smash it... because you will probably pull your groin'.

So, I am going into the last game thinking *I am fit enough to start, but I need to kind of hold back a small bit.* It was my right groin, so I was thinking if I can get something on my left foot or my head, I would have been a lot happier one-on-one with the keeper. Lo and behold, I scored the first goal that night with my head.

I remember getting it to the left hand side, just bringing it across to the mid and passing the ball across to Roy O'Donovan.

I got myself into the box… Roy put a great ball in and I got in between the two Derry centre-halves and… BANG… that was it. I think that really steadied our nerves.

We needed to win that game to be crowned champions. Derry just needed to draw that game. We never had any thought but to go out, start on the front foot and try to get into a lead to win that game. Scoring that goal personally for me was fantastic.

All of my family, friends and loved ones, they were all there. It was my local club. They were all in the stadium for the last night of the Shed. That really calmed us down and led onto a momentous night. But it is definitely for me the game that will live long in the memory.

We felt going into the 2005 season that we were going to win it.

We weren't shouting it from the rooftops, but we had a quiet confidence that we were going to win the league that year. It was probably not my greatest season goals-wise and continuous game-wise, but it all clicked because as a group and as a whole, we were really on it that year.

We had a strong base of Cork players and a mixture of lads who weren't from Cork. We had Pat Dolan in that pre-season… he would have been there the previous season also. There were ingredients there that we knew, and then just before the start of the season there was a shake-up. Pat Dolan was told he was going to be sacked, Damien Richardson was coming in.

I never forget that day in Rochestown Park.

There was a meeting and we never saw it coming. It was obviously stuff behind the scenes that we didn't know about. We were focused on getting pre-season over with and starting the season on a high. But Rico came in and did really well. He was one of those characters who came in, saw the talent that we had and said 'lads, just go out and express yourselves, go out and play football'. We did that.

Rico kind of had that relaxed manner about him. He could lose the rag as well, and you knew if he was about to burst. But the majority of the time he had that relaxed manner about him. He definitely knew the squad of players that he had and he gave us that freedom to go out and express ourselves. There was never a constraint that you had to play this one role and you couldn't go out past the realms of that specific job.

He just gave lads freedom. Probably prior to that, I knew him as a guy on TV who would be saying them big words and spouting that big chat. But when he came in, his character all came into one. He was well able to man-manage and manage that team of players.

Looking at it, if I was coming in as a manager with that wealth of talent that you are inheriting, it would probably be the same bill; there is no point in going in trying to re-invent the wheel, getting these last to do things they weren't used to doing. We all had our habits and things we had built up over the years.

There were things we were good at and some things we weren't good at... and Rico highlighted the things we were good at and said go out and do it. So, it was refreshing from the balance of Pat going and Damien coming in, that balance could have thrown everyone off as well, if it was the wrong manager or personality

There were some fantastic characters and there were leaders all over the pitch. The Cork base of players made it special as well. We all knew what we were up against... expectation of fans, expectation of parents, relatives and all that. I think if you are outside or unless you have lived in the city or played for the club more than two or three years, you don't really get it. Somebody coming in doesn't know how much it actually means. But we all knew what it meant and that was probably the highlight of that season.

Kevin Doyle started the 2005 season and he went to England halfway through. It was just before the European games started, so it was quite early on. We were down Kevin for more than half that season. He was a big loss, but you had the likes of Denis Behan and Neale Fenn... Roy O'Donovan who could play up front. We had a massive array of attacking talent. But definitely the foundations for us was Mick Devine and the back four.

I think that year, more than any other, we didn't score a massive amount of goals, but the defence was rock solid. You had Mick Devine there. You had Alan Bennett and Dan Murray, who sparked up that partnership. You had Hoggy (Neal

Horgan) on the right and Danny Murphy, the Cockney Rebel, on the left. Every week the back four and 'keeper… they knew their jobs and how they liked to play.

The unit, they knew it like the back of their hands. There was a lot of 1-0 wins. We probably won games 2-0, 3-1 or 3-2, but there were a lot where it was 1-0. It was 1-0, because we scored a goal and then the lads did their jobs at the back and kept a clean sheet.

If we had a five-a-side, there could be Dan or Benno on either side. Then you are talking Hoggy and Danny, Joe Gamble, Neale Fenn, Roy O'Donovan, Georgie, myself. We had so much talent. We used to actually joke that training was actually harder than matches and we used to kick lumps out of each other. There was never animosity about if Denis Behan was starting ahead of me; we all had that confidence about us and team spirit.

It is a fact that some of our training sessions used to be harder than the games. The games used to be a release… *go out and enjoy yourself and play*. But as well as the leaders that we had, we had lads who had really, *really* high expectations and high standards. If your touch was off or if you weren't at it, you were just left behind really.

There was enough fellas to tell you that you are not at it today. I think it was a really good balance of fellas who wanted to win so badly, who had the skill level and intensity. But also, there was never a lack of anything in a training session. It is a funny thing to think back about the plethora of talent we had at this stage.

Leading into the Derry game, we would have had a training session, where we were in good spirits and quietly confident we would go on and win that game. Obviously, there was anxiety and stuff bubbling underneath that wouldn't come up. Liam Kearney would have been a fiery character anyway.

We were playing a five-a-side game, two touch or whatever it was. We were all having fun, plenty of goals and a small kind of a pitch. Stuff that really got us focused and on our toes about the game coming up. Kearney whipped a cross in and thought it took a deflection off somebody. Rico gave a goal-kick… we had all moved on talking for 15 or 20 seconds and then… we hear this kind of noise.

I just looked back and Liam Kearney had lost his head.

He was basically squaring up to Rico, saying he was adamant it was a corner-kick. It was like someone took all his toys off him in the pram and said he was never getting them back. He just lost it… all his emotion came out. The more we were listening to it, the more we're thinking this is going to boil over. Rico must have been thinking *steady on here, you are getting closer to me…* and the steam coming out of his ears.

Only for the fact we as players fell on the floor laughing and found it the funniest thing ever, then the emotions subsided. It is something that we always bring up. But that was another thing where a player like Kearney had to release that energy… then relax and get into the game. Being a good manager, you need to know which guy might need a kick in the arse, and which guy might need an arm around him to tell him he is the best player ever and you love him and all that.

That was just a funny memory for me leading into the game.

Before we went out onto the pitch, we obviously knew that the atmosphere was going to be electric. We didn't realise there was going to be that many people there as we turned up. As we went out to warm up… normally for the warm up there might be only a couple of hundred people coming in early, reading the programme and watching. But there were thousands there that night, so it felt like the game was about to kick off when we were walking out to actually go and warm up.

In the dressing-room, Derek Coughlan stood up and said his bit in his deep Cork voice and his big frame. Everyone just stood up. What he said was what it meant to him and what it meant to the Cork people and the fans outside. It was a moment where the hairs are standing up on the back of your neck and we were going out ready to go to war basically after the rousing speech from Derek.

I remember when we won it… I don't know where my jersey went as I threw it somewhere And you are looking around for the faces, your family to get the hug.

Selections would have been a big thing leading into that game. Paddy McCourt was been a fella you could roll the ball to as a Derry goalkeeper and he could have taken the whole team on and put the ball in the net. He was that kind of a player, he was just phenomenal. We played against Derry a few times leading into that game during that season, and we knew how good he was and they were tough battles.

There was a bit of needle there between the teams. Even though the fans got on superbly well, and even after Derry fans had lost that night there was no animosity or ill feeling. But Paddy McCourt was named on the bench… right before we got the team sheet, and that was a massive plus for us.

Whether he wasn't fit, or if Stephen Kenny felt someone else could do the job better, I don't know, but we felt as a team that was a big turning point. Paddy came on and had a guilt-edged chance… a header right at the far post, and Mick Devine made an unbelievable save that was a pivotal moment in that game that probably doesn't get highlighted as much as me scoring that goal or Kearney scoring the second goal

I remember the lads bought the cup into the Shed at the end of the game. I totally missed that, as I was off with friends and family. Then I went into the changing room, but the lads had come back to say they were all in the Shed celebrating with the fans. When we won the league in Cork that night, I remember we probably didn't put our hands in our pockets for three or four weeks after that.

Anywhere in Cork we went, there were people pulling us into shops, saying pick whatever ye want. In December of the 2005 season I turned on the Christmas lights in Cork city centre. That is how much of a pedestal we were up on. It was a momentous occasion.

It definitely encapsulates every kind of emotion that you ever would face as a footballer. That night, it just all clicked and they were great emotions. Twenty years I was a footballer, and the majority of that time was with Cork City in one spell and then another spell. It is always Cork City for me.

BILLY WOODS

CORK CITY 1 ★ APOLLON LIMASSOL 0
UEFA Champions League
First Qualifying Round First Leg
Turner's Cross
JULY 12, 2006

Billy Woods shoots to score Cork's first goal against Apallon Limassol at Turner's Cross.

★ **CORK CITY:** M Devine; N Horgan, A Bennett, D Murray, D Murphy, R O'Donovan, C O'Brien, J Gamble, **B Woods**, N Fenn, D Behan. Sub: C Lordan for Behan

★ **APOLLON LIMASSOL:** A Chvalovsky; L Alvarez, R Michalski, G Merkis, A Solomou, B Andone, M Karim, J Arig, M Barun, L Sosin, M Hamadi. Subs: J Paiva for Hamadi, M Hawar for Solomou, A Alves for Andone.

THE ACTION

A SUPERB FINISH from Billy Woods was enough to give Cork City the advantage after the first leg of their UEFA Champions League first qualifying round tie against Apollon Limassol of Cyprus at Turner's Cross.

Picking up the ball from a neat pass by Joe Gamble, Billy Woods fired home from the edge of the box. Shortly beforehand, the home side forced a save from Chvalovsky in the Apollon goal through a Danny Murphy effort.

Denis Behan also went close to scoring from a free kick, while Woods and Roy O'Donovan also had chances before the game took that dramatic twist, with the only goal of the night arriving just past the hour mark in the contest.

Apollon went very close to getting an equaliser, when skipper and Poland international Lukasz Sosin saw his curling free kick come back off the post.

This was a first defeat in 27 matches for the Cypriot champions. The second leg of this tie was played the following week in Cyprus, with City ultimately winning 2-1 on aggregate thanks to a header by Dan Murray, to set up a tie in the following round with Red Star Belgrade.

★★★★★

66

ONE OF MY favourite games for Cork City was when we played Apollon Limassol at Turner's Cross in the Champions League Qualifying Round.

On a glorious night, we won 1-0 and I was lucky enough to score the only goal. Both my parents attended the game; my wife was at home watching the game live on TV with our newborn son Ryan.

That night to me was probably one of the best nights of my career. To share that with my parents, my wife and son was fantastic. To play for Cork City, the team you love in such a big game at that stage of my career was special to me. The crowd, the noise, friends and family all there… and playing for your hometown club was special.

Bar the redevelopment of the Shed end there was a full house for this Champions League tie. Looking back now, it was simply a great experience. We had a bit of an up and down season in 2006; we had lost a couple of players after the league winning season to our rivals and George O' Callaghan had a disagreement with our manager Damien Richardson.

We were working off a small pool of players. We were in contention for the league, but I don't think we were ever going to win it that year, even though we had a group of high-quality players that were committed, professional and experienced.

Coming into the tie it was difficult to know what to expect against our Cypriot opponents. We had been given some information on them by the management team but this wasn't a period when opposition analysis was used greatly. But once the game started, we knew that we had an opportunity to beat them.

The first-half was particularly tight. I had a long-range strike in the second-half, which the 'keeper saved. The goal itself came from Joe Gamble winning the ball high in midfield and turning over possession in a dangerous area. He played the ball to me, as I had come in from the left wing into an area where it was difficult for the full-back to come out.

I took the ball in field and I remember at the time that I thought on my first touch that I would be closed down, but the defenders stood off, and I was able to manipulate the ball onto my stronger right foot and whip it high into the keeper's left hand corner of the goal.

The feeling was simply elation with my teammates. We did the 'Bebeto' celebration right in front of my parents… I have pictures of this at home in the attic, and it's something that I really look back on with great memories. Once we scored the goal, we were pretty comfortable and went onto win.

It was special for me to have my late mother come and watch her son play in a European game at Turner's Cross, on a fantastic summers evening, and to get a great result for the club. In football there are so many days when it just doesn't happen either for you or the team, but your parents are there supporting you through thick and thin, so it was special to have that moment with them.

Cork City was my club since 1984. I would go to watch games, and then to end up playing for so long for them, and winning every trophy in Ireland was the highlight of my career. When you are from Cork playing for your team and it is your club, that means so much more. Damien Richardson at the time was the manager. I have a lot of time and respect for Damien. He was and is a gentleman.

I worked with him for over seven years. He signed me after I came home from the UK and gave me my debut. He left and took over Shelbourne, and at Shamrock Rovers I played three seasons under him before he returned to Cork for his second spell. He instilled confidence in the players, and he had a fundamental belief in people and their ability.

His message was simple and, on reflection, he didn't need to complicate the game. He had excellent players whom he wanted to express themselves through hard work.

Players like Roy O'Donovan, who was hitting an amazing spell between that and the following season. It was a brilliant team to play in for me. We won the league in 2005 and then we lost a couple of players. We won the FAI Cup in 2007 and Setanta Cup in '08. So, you had characters there that were the backbone of Cork City for this period.

Joe Gamble was a brilliant player, and Neale Fenn was such a natural talent. Neal Horgan, Mick Devine, Danny Murphy, Dan Murray, Alan Bennett, Cillian Lordan, Colin O'Brien, Denis Behan… they were just superb characters to play with and great people to train with. They set high standards every day and they were committed to the club.

The level of professionalism was excellent. There were a couple of turbulent spells but Brian Lennox then became the chairman and did a trojan job, and an amazing amount of work with the likes of Liam Murphy. From Liam to Pat Dolan and Damien Richardson, they were committed to pushing the club on and did so successfully.

Liam Murphy brought George and John O'Flynn back from the UK. Pat brought in Liam Kearney, while Damien brought in Roy O'Donovan. This injection into the team of Cork boys playing at home in front of their families and full of confidence brought the club to the next level. You had young kids in the team, and me being one of the elder statesmen of the side at the time, it was brilliant to see lads who had ultra-confidence in themselves. During this period between 2003 and '07 we had Kevin Doyle, Shane Long, Joe, Alan Bennett and David Meyler, who would have great careers in the UK and go on to play for Ireland.

The aim for any player who starts out in a career is to test themselves at the highest level and play against the best players. We were fortunate at Cork City to have great runs in Europe. We had fantastic runs in Europe under Pat Dolan, Damien Richardson and later John Caulfield.

There have been bigger nights in the club's history than this game, but that night is special to me. It is not often that you get to play in Europe. It doesn't happen every year and it is very difficult to beat teams. Irish clubs at times went into games with an inferiority complex. Pat Dolan changed this mind-set for the group of players in Cork during our 2004 run. He was relentless in his belief that Irish clubs could compete in Europe.

In the next round after that game, we played Red Star Belgrade and if we had beaten Red Star, we would have faced AC Milan after that in 2006. That would have been amazing. In the second leg in Cyprus, we drew 1-1 with Dan Murray getting a brilliant header and we went through on aggregate 2-1. After the game, coming down the tunnel, Danny Murphy and Joe Gamble were both sent off for fighting. They ended up in a row with some security members of Apollon Limassol and there was a massive punch up.

We actually went into the first home leg of the Red Star Belgrade tie without Danny and Joe, while John O'Flynn was missing also. So, we were three players down. That was very challenging for us, because we had a small squad at the time really. It was still great to play in Europe against teams of that quality.

It is very difficult to pick out one game from my career. Obviously winning leagues and cups was the pinnacle of my Cork City career. But from a personal point of view years later, to be able to celebrate scoring in front of your parents, your wife and newborn baby is something that I am proud of. At that stage of my career, I was 32 and knew that games like this would become less frequent for me.

People like Jerry Harris made the club what it is… the amount of work they did off the pitch, incredible unseen work and to share that win with people that you appreciate everyday was just special, really.

Playing in Europe is a great reward for having a good season the previous year. That is where Cork City should be. It needs to be competing in Europe year-in and year-out. We were fortunate to have that run of years.

European football is the pinnacle, and I was fortunate to share it with some amazing people, great players and, fortunately, people I count as friends.

GRAHAM CUMMINS

SHELBOURNE 1 ★ CORK CITY 2
League Of Ireland First Division
Tolka Park
OCTOBER 29, 2011

Graham Cummins celebrates after scoring Cork's second and winning goal against Shelbourne at Tolka Park.

★ **SHELBOURNE:** D Delany; G Matthews, A Boyle, I Ryan, S Byrne, B McGill, J Sullivan, D Cassidy, K Dawson, B Clancy; P Hughes. Subs: P Gorman for Hughes, C Byrne for Clancy, C Mulhall for McGill.

★ **CORK CITY:** M McNulty; N Horgan, G Kavanagh, K Spillane, D Murphy; G Morrissey, G O'Halloran, S Duggan, D Horgan, D O'Neill, **G Cummins**. Subs: V Sullivan for O'Neill, D O'Brien for Kavanagh, I Turner for D Horgan.

THE ACTION

COURTESY OF A memorable 94th minute winner by Graham Cummins, Cork City won the League Of Ireland First Division title in the most dramatic of circumstances against Shelbourne at Tolka Park.

While the club had won a Premier Division league title in 2005, the outpouring of emotion from both City fans and players surpassed the celebrations of that November night six years previously. In addition, the fact that it was in a title decider against Shelbourne, and on their home turf also, made the taste of victory all the sweeter for City supporters.

With just seconds remaining on the clock, Cummins wrote his name into club folklore by heading in from a Derek O'Brien cross.

Although Shels laid siege to the opposition goal during the opening half of play, it was City who went in front courtesy of a drilled finish by Daryl Horgan.

Shelbourne equalised in the 28th minute. Philly Hughes showed tremendous vision to play a defence-splitting pass for David Cassidy, who slotted the ball past City goalkeeper Mark McNulty.

In a contest which was effectively a cup final, the second-half was not as frantic, but remained just as captivating. When it appeared as though a draw was on the cards, with just seconds remaining Cummins and City struck.

★★★★★

66

THAT IS THE pinnacle for me, that game, and it is definitely the highlight of my career. I have had good moments, such as scoring at Ibrox, scoring against Celtic and playing in Celtic Park. When I was six or seven, if you said to me you'd get to play against Rangers, play at Celtic Park, I would have thought that would be as good as it ever got for me.

But definitely that game in 2011 probably was the thing that made me have a good relationship with Cork City fans. Hopefully, I always will have. It is something that will stick in the memory, kind of putting your name down in history, I feel now. When you mention the role FORAS played as well, it means a lot.

I have said it on numerous occasions that I wasn't playing well that night. I think nerves got the better of me; I was always a player who had a lot of nerves and anxiety that kind of way. I just wanted to see the finishing goal. You go preparing for the best scenario afterwards… you never think of the worst.

I don't think we ever went up there thinking that if we drew, then we will be happy. I wouldn't have been happy drawing and leaving that there. So, you are visualising your nights out that week and what you are going to be doing. When it was 1-1, and especially the way the game was going, Shels were well on top of us and Nults made a lot of saves in the first-half in particular.

I can still remember Derek O'Brien crossing the ball and getting my head onto it. It was probably one of the best headers I have ever had… and I scored a lot of headers. Definitely in terms of importance, but also in terms of technique. I remember going onto the bus afterwards and Tommy Dunne was watching the goal. He said it was an unbelievable header… because the ball was actually behind me, and I had never realised that at the time.

Not behind me as in my head, but I had to go backwards to change my neck movement, and I had to get a lot of power in my actual neck. I just thought that it was a straightforward header. So, I was actually quite proud of that. When I scored, I just ran over to the crowd and I really did think there was still 10 or 11 minutes left. Maybe if I had known at the time that it was that last kick of the game, I probably would have been a lot more nervous.

If you watch the goal back, we are actually very patient in our build up play. We did play the right way that year. Our lead up to that goal was great, we didn't just launch the ball into the box. It wasn't launch the ball into the box and see what happens, it was very patient play.

We only lost one game that season, I think it was Waterford at home. We came back after the break and we beat Shels at home 4-1, but a few weeks later we drew with Wexford at home. But towards the end of the season, we were playing games and thinking Shels might just drop points.

I remember we beat Salthill up in Salthill and then Shels lost to Waterford in the RSC. We had one more game at home after that against Longford in the second last game of the season. Then the momentum swung.

We would have been disappointed just to get promoted. I never understand that in England, where clubs are happy just to get promoted. For me it was about winning the title. I have a promotion with Rochdale, but it means absolutely nothing to me because it was just a promotion. I didn't play the next year, so maybe that is why. I feel it doesn't mean anything if you don't win something.

After we drew with Wexford, I thought it was over. Waterford were a very good team and that was the big game… Shels dropped points at home unexpectedly. It was in our hands then. That is all we wanted. I know Shels had the advantage of being allowed to draw the game but, in fairness to them, that night in the first-half they were well on top. I think sometimes it's easier to be the chaser than the chased, because all of the pressure was on Shels. There was nothing really on us… we just went out and we kept winning every week. We did put pressure on ourselves there is no doubt about that, but I think all Cork City fans were just thinking, *look, if we can get promoted that would be great.* But all of the players in the dressing-room were still thinking, *lets beat them, let's beat them!*

We only lost one game that season. We played Shels three times that year. We drew in Tolka Park previously and we also beat them 4-1 in Turner's Cross. We knew we were the better side when you can beat your rivals, when you have not lost to them and beaten them 4-1. So really, it would have been a bit of a travesty if we had drawn that night and Shels had won the league having never beaten us and us absolutely battering them in Turner's Cross.

We had a good blend of experience. Danny Murphy was in there and Davin O'Neill… a lot of lads who had won titles before. There was a very good understanding. We lost the League Cup final that year to Derry City and I think we were very unlucky to lose that one. So, there was always belief that we had a good team. In fairness to Tommy Dunne, I thought he was an excellent coach. The way he trained us, everyone knew our jobs. Like we knew everything we were doing going out on the pitch. We would analyse a game on a Monday morning and there would be more negatives than positives even when we won.

I think Tommy Dunne's role was massive because when you think of it, he took the job from nothing at the start. He had been Roddy Collins' assistant to the Premier Division side before the club went bust basically. Tommy took over and he was so strict on lads. A lot of training was just repetitive all the time, but you knew exactly what you were doing.

While some managers were working on different things every day, he made sure you were an expert at what you were doing, and what you needed to do. So that is when I look at him and go like, *he had passing drills to death...* but we could pass the ball really good come a Friday night. We were not doing something that we were not practicing.

I think when we went up to the Premier Division, probably the expectations with City, and rightly so, was so high. That fans just expected him to just win the league. But it takes a long time to get going and to get players. In the First Division there were a lot of Cork lads in terms of recruitment, but for the Premier Division you need more than just one location to win this division. You can't keep lads unless it is Dublin, with a very big population. I think Tommy was massive and he was certainly massive in my career, anyway.

When you look at that Cork City team now, you had the likes of Daryl Horgan, Gearóid Morrissey, Shane Duggan, Danny Murphy, Neal Horgan... Nults in goal. I know they were young at the time, but that was a hell of a team and that was a really good side we managed to string together.

I would imagine Tommy Dunne didn't have a massive budget at the time. So, it was a really good team. In terms of characteristics, we always just believed and we always seemed to enjoy things. We had a good blend of lads who wanted to mess around and lads who wanted to be professional. Neal Horgan had a big influence on the dressing-room. I know at the time he was playing GAA and would miss some games, with us, but his calming influence was a big thing.

I played well the season before and I knew there was interest in me all of the time. I always say those years were my best years because football wasn't a job, it was just playing. I was living at home and I was going to college. Football was second to me, it was never something that was paying my bills or anything like that.

It was something for me that helped to go to restaurants or eat food; it was never going towards an electricity bill. So, they were great times. Then it changes when you get older and it becomes a job. There was good players around me and everything I hit that year just seemed to go into the back of the net.

I was always playing with a confidence because my head was like, *I will score this week*. I always thought one in two was a great ratio, so if I scored one week I think the following week I don't need to score. But then I would score again and it relieved the pressure. I never had pressure because I kept scoring and would think, *I have a free game next week*. Although I remember I started that season really badly, I think it was my fourth or fifth game before I actually scored.

It was a great bus trip back home. We stopped in Abbeyleix, in a pub there and we had a few drinks with the fans. Watching the video the next morning as well… it was just a great feeling, really. I always feel that away games can be that bit more special, and for the supporters, they enjoyed the whole trip.

I know with the 2005 title win the city was unbelievable, but I imagine that day in 2011 was special for fans in terms of they all travelled up together, they spent the whole day together… went for a few drinks in Dublin. I am speaking from my own experience because my wife went up and my family, my mam and dad, they all went together.

They were probably talking about the game the whole way up. Whereas if you were in Turner's Cross, you are not meeting up with your family until maybe half an hour before the game. Then you are talking about what might happen if you win.

I am enjoying life as a football journalist now.

Sometimes, you see things and go… *am I being a bit harsh?* Because I could be very harsh on myself. As a player you might be very harsh on yourself and then you might go, *why can't I be harsh on them now?* But you try and be fair always.

But I really do enjoy it, in terms of going to matches without having that pressure of getting scrutinised for every single thing. I find it more enjoyable now on a Friday night as I don't have that panic going into a ground.

It is a lot more relaxed.

99

GARRY BUCKLEY

DERRY CITY 0 ★ CORK CITY 1
League Of Ireland Premier Division
Brandywell Stadium
SEPTEMBER 7, 2012

Garry Buckley celebrates after scoring Cork's first goal in the FAI Cup semi-final against Limerick at Turner's Cross.

★ **DERRY CITY:** G Doherty; S Madden, S McEleney, R McBride, D McCaffrey, P McEleney, R Higgins, B Molloy, S McLaughlin, C Murphy, D McDaid. Subs: M Farren for Murphy, M Brolly for P McEleney.

★ **CORK CITY:** M McNulty; G Kavanagh, K Murray, K Spillane, D Murphy, **G Buckley**, I Turner, G Morrissey, S Duggan, D O'Neill, V Sullivan. Subs: K Parker for Sullivan, K Quinn for O'Neill, S Kenny for Turner.

THE ACTION

CORK CITY CAME away from The Brandywell with all three points following a resolute display against Derry City.

The club's former under-19 double-winning captain Garry Buckley got all of the plaudits, having being drafted into midfield in the absence of Daryl Horgan and heading into the back of the net for the only goal on the night.

Derry began strongly and Ruaidhri Higgins had an effort saved by Cork goalkeeper Mark McNulty in the third minute, and he was also called into action to save from Patrick McEleney later in the first-half.

The Candystripes threatened again on 15 minutes, but Stephen McLaughlin's free kick was gathered comfortably by McNulty. City mustered their first chance on target seven minutes later, when Gerard Doherty tipped Shane Duggan's header on to the crossbar, and then McNulty was again on top form as he deflected an effort from midfielder McEleney around his post.

Derry continued to apply plenty of attacking pressure into the second-half. Barry Molloy and Conor Murphy both had decent chances, but the Cork back line held firm. However, the fixture took a definite turn in City's direction with 22 minutes remaining. Davin O'Neill broke forward and found himself clear on goal with only Doherty to beat, but the 'keeper saved well from the Cork No 9, conceding a corner. Then Buckley was on hand to head the resulting set-piece to the back of the net, breaking the deadlock and firing City ahead in the process.

McNulty kept his side in front when David McDaid might have levelled matters six minutes later, and the night ended in further disappointment for Declan Devine and his men when Ryan McBride saw a straight red card after a two-footed tackle on Buckley in added time.

★★★★★

"

THE GAME THAT defined me was my league debut. It kick-started my career. Without that game, I mightn't have gotten another opportunity. Without that game, who knows what would have happened.

It was early September of 2012. Back then we had a great under-19s team and there were a lot of us in the first team. There was talk of 'are we going to be kept on'… and this and that. I got an opportunity to play a game as there was a few injuries. I played in midfield up in Derry. I had just turned 19 at the time. There was one or two other lads who were on the team who were great players… and they were going out on loan, and fizzling away.

It was kind of make-or-break time for me.

I actually scored the winning goal on my debut up in the Brandywell! I got my first professional contract out of that. From there then, it kicked on… I got a bit of confidence in myself more and I never looked back, really. That was defining moment in my career because it could have gone either way then.

Tommy Dunne mightn't have given me an opportunity or mightn't have given me a chance. I always feel like that game, that was my opportunity and I took it. It was 0-0 and I think I was playing defensive midfield with Colin Healy and Gearóid Morrissey. Shane Duggan was injured at the time.

Early in the second-half a corner came in. I remember Kevin Murray at the back post headed towards goal. But it landed in the six-yard box and I just headed it into the top corner. It was a mad feeling getting my first professional goal… and the winner in the end. I actually had a great game overall, which was most pleasing for me. From there, I gained Tommy's confidence and he knew that he could trust me.

You get opportunities in football and that was my one. I knew I had to take it and, thankfully, I did on the day.

We were mad underdogs in that game as well. The crowd was unbelievable and they really got behind their team. We were hanging on for ages, blocks on the line and stuff like that. We stayed in the game and I scored that goal… and we stuck it out.

It was a great game. Afterwards, I remember it was some feeling. I just couldn't believe it that I actually scored for the Cork City senior team. It was dream stuff. I look back on those times as unbelievable. I can't thank Tommy Dunne enough for the opportunity. My hard work had also paid off in the end.

Growing up, all I ever wanted to do was play for Cork City.

My brother played for Cork City years before me and he wore the No 26 jersey as well. So, there was a bit of pride in that number. I had always gone to Cork City matches, even as a young teenager with my dad. All I ever wanted to do was play for Cork… even when I was playing for Leeds underage, I knew I wanted to leave when I was 16 or 17 and wanted to play for Cork City Youths.

I wanted to go through that process. I was tunnel-visioned in that way… that is what I wanted to do.

I trained with the City first team for months before that. There were other boys getting more opportunities than me, but I stuck it out and stayed as fit as I could… remained dedicated, did the gym work, and didn't get up to bad stuff off the pitch.

Luckily, I got my opportunity and I took it. That was a catalyst for my career for Cork City. I was young at the time, I was making benches but very inexperienced.

We had Daryl Horgan, Shane Duggan, Gearóid Morrissey, Colin Healy, Dan Murray… Danny Murphy was there, Vinny Sullivan, Davin O'Neill. We had a very good eleven. There was a good team and a very good set of players, and they went on in the years after that and showed their quality.

Colin Healy was still unbelievable years after that as well. Colin was well respected in the dressing-room. He was a very strong character. Not necessarily shouting and roaring, but he led by example. I think he always had to be a Cork City manager. You could always see he had great passion for the club and for the city. For me as a Cork City supporter, it is great to see him doing so well.

When John Caulfield came in then, he really took it by the scruff of the neck… obviously it went full-time and pushed the club on even more. Tommy was a very good coach I thought, and knew what he was talking about. A bit mad, but I suppose every manager has their mad traits. I really liked Tommy and got on well with him.

The club was going through a transition then, getting a bit of stability on and off the pitch. Everybody in the league wants to make Europe every year.

Realistically for us, it was more of a dream rather than an expectation. Tommy definitely consolidated the club. Obviously, it didn't work out in the end for him. But the club can definitely thank him for his services and what he did for the club, getting them up and staying up. The success that happened afterwards, he is definitely a part of that.

He brought players to the club that were a part of that. Johnny Dunleavy was part of that and Gearóid Morrissey was part of that. I was part of that.

I was just leaving school at the time and John Caulfield was going full-time. It was music to my ears to be honest. All I wanted to do was to be a footballer, and it suited me down to the ground to go full time… no worries, still living at home and stuff like that. John put that professional mentality on it, that if you are going to do it you want to do it right. No excuses… train like a footballer and stuff like that.

Your focus is all on football… that was instilled in all of us. There was nobody really working, maybe Dan Murray a bit at the time

All of our focus was on football and I think that is why we did so well… there was no distractions. It was a dream. I was at the title winning game in 2005 and I was at the FAI Cup in 2007. What I wanted to do is, I wanted to be out there myself.

The 2016 FAI Cup final… to lose in the cup final the year before, come second in the league twice and it's like… *are we ever going to win a trophy?* All I ever wanted to do was win a league with Cork City. The 2005 league was a special night, even for me being in the crowd. I was only 11 years old at the time, on my dad's shoulders on the pitch

So you are thinking to yourself is all of this hard work going to pay off ? The feeling of Seánie hitting the back of that net in that game was probably the best feeling I have ever had in football, and probably still is right now. To know that the game is over and we are going to get our hands on our first trophy. As a team, all of us had been through a lot, so that was definitely my favourite game… probably still is as well.

Every year we had records that we could have beaten and stuff like that. The first Cork team to do the double… the first Cork team to do back-to-back cup finals. You'd talk about that team from 2005 and how good that team was… getting to two cup finals in three years and winning the league.

To think we actually had a bit more success than them is mad, considering how much I put them on a pedestal when I was young. It is great times you look back on. I am so thankful that we won so much as we did. All of the hard work paid off.

Look at Seánie Maguire, he was a bit unknown until John Caulfield signed him up. So that goes on everywhere. Everyone gets their chance somewhere and managers give an opportunity. It just happened that Tommy Dunne gave me my opportunity. Hopefully, I have made Tommy proud that he kick-started my career.

Not just Tommy, but John Caulfield further kick-started my career too at the time. When John came in, I was a bit of an unknown still. I had probably 30 or 40 appearances in the league, but John kind of gave me a kick… and made me from a good player, to a very good player. I always thank my managers for everything.

Also, the likes of Stuart Ashton, Paul Bowdren and John Cotter, they all played their part for me and I am hoping that I played my part for them too. To be honest, every minute was unbelievable. All I ever wanted to do was to play and win with Cork City, and I've done that and more than I ever thought.

Then, we didn't have a great season and I left. The club moved on… and I moved on, it was just one of those things. Many other players in the club who are heroes and legends moved on to other clubs too. But I look back with great pride being a Corkman and winning the double. I was told I was the first Northsider to captain the club… in a couple of games towards the end.

That fills me with great pride as well. Every moment of it, there was good times and bad times. But ninety-nine percent of the time, they were all great times because we won so much and we were competing. All the lads, to be fair, everyone in our dressing-room was spot on.

The banter and stuff going on, you'd miss that.

Looking back as a Corkman having all those medals with Cork City, I'll never forget them obviously. I hope the club are up next year. Maybe I might be back in Turner's Cross playing against them.

When it is going well, there is absolutely no club in the country that can compete with the fans support at Cork City. The crowds have been good in 2022 in the First Division, so they see the progress and, thankfully, they are getting behind the team.

It was like the early part of the John Caulfield years as well, they were getting behind them. Hopefully, that can continue because Cork needs and the country needs a good, strong Cork City team absolutely.

I am really enjoying it now in Sligo. I kind of came up into an unknown leaving Cork for the first time. But from the minute I have been here, Sligo Rovers have been fantastic to me. They really looked after me off the pitch… accommodation and anything I needed.

They really made me feel like I was at home away from home. I feel settled here now in Sligo. We had a really good season in 2021, coming third, and the two years I have been here we have got into Europe, so that is a great achievement.

I can't have any complaints on and off the pitch here. I am really settled now. I have had a child here in Sligo… a Sligo baby and the misses is happy. So, I have no complaints and why would I have complaints being a professional footballer.

In the grand scheme of things, it is a great job to have.

COLIN HEALY

CORK CITY 1 ★ ST PATRICK'S ATHLETIC 0
League Of Ireland Premier Division
Turner's Cross
AUGUST 8, 2014

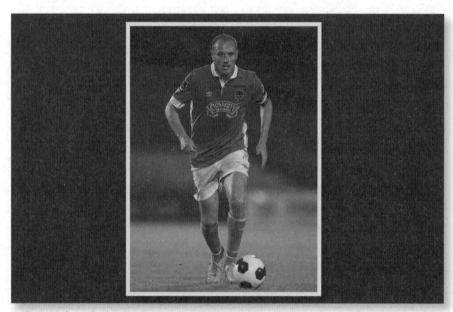

Colin Healy in typical style on the ball at Turner's Cross.

★ **CORK CITY:** M McNulty; J Dunleavy, D Murray, M McSweeney, R Gaynor, L Kearney, G Morrissey, **C Healy**, B Dennehy, M O'Sullivan, J O'Flynn. Subs: D Morrissey for Kearney, J O'Shea for O'Flynn, D O'Leary for Dennehy.

★ **ST PATRICK'S ATHLETIC:** B Clarke; C McCormack, K Browne, K Brennan, I Bermingham, C Byrne, K Fahey, M Quigley, G Bolger, A Greene; C Fagan. Sub: G O'Brien for Greene.

THE ACTION

A SENSATIONAL OVERHEAD kick from Colin Healy breathed new life into the 2014 League of Ireland Premier Division title race for Cork City, as they won an enthralling encounter against St Patrick's Athletic.

After one of the greatest goals that Turner's Cross has ever witnessed, the victory saw City move to within four points of league leaders Dundalk.

The home side commenced strongly and Dan Murray forced St Pat's goalkeeper Brendan Clarke into a decent save. The return of Keith Fahey was a massive boost for the Dublin side, with the Irish international forcing a good stop out of City goalkeeper Mark McNulty early into the second-half.

Danny Morrissey went close for Cork shortly afterwards from a Mark O'Sullivan cross, but his effort was somehow kept out. At the other end, Pat's went agonisingly close to scoring through a Conan Byrne shot that came back off the post.

With the game approaching the final 10 minutes, Pat's were then reduced to 10 men as Mark Quigley saw red for a second yellow card. That was before City scored what turned out to be a stunning winner. From a corner kick, Healy was provided with the opportunity to fire home spectacularly and seal a valuable three points for the Rebel Army.

★★★★★

"

I GOT THAT goal against St Pats, an overhead kick. Obviously, we went on to win that game, and we were fighting for the league at that time as well. We were going for the title that year.

We were playing against a very good St Pat's team that had the likes of Greg Bolger and Keith Fahey. We needed to win. We didn't go on to win the league, but we came very, very close that year.

It just sticks out because it was an important game and obviously, I got that goal. There would have been other games as well. We had the FAI Cup final when Seánie Maguire got that winner. That was important and it was my last game.

For some reason, the Pat's game is in my head because every time it comes around, people talk about that goal. I didn't score many goals.

We started well. I think people knew what we were about, and we were difficult to play against. We were aggressive, we were hard working… and we had a good team spirit. That grew stronger and *stronger*. We were pushing and we wanted to get the win, we wanted to get the three points.

Billy Dennehy put one in, and I think Mark O'Sullivan went up for a header. It came up in the air and it is probably one of those, that you just give it a go.

Listen, it came off. Other times it probably wouldn't have had. But it came off and we got the three points. It gave us some confidence going into the last few games. It gave us that confidence that we could go and beat these teams. It was a great three points for us. The crowds were in and the place was hopping.

They had Bolger, Brennan and Fahey in the middle of the park. Then there was myself, Gearóid and Bucks. It was always going to be a difficult one there. But I think we got the better of them that night, and it was a big three points.

It probably showed us that we could go on and do something. As the years went on, the boys did go and do that. That was John Caulfield's first year and things clicked together quickly. We brought in some good players and we bought into it. We were very strong and went on.

Pat's won the league the previous year. In 2014, you could see why City went on to win the double and won the cups, because there was a lot of work done. The fans were in… big crowds were in. The team got stronger and stronger every year.

You could see where the club was going. The only thing was, I was probably at the other end of my career. I was coming towards the end. I wasn't starting off like Gearóid, Bucks and some of the younger players. I enjoyed it and to win the FAI Cup on my last appearance for the club was nice to finish off with.

We had some good senior players within that dressing-room the first year. John Caulfield brought in some lads from the Munster Senior League and there was a good work ethic. We went very close. Unfortunately, we were pipped by a very good side in Dundalk. Nobody thought we were going to go so close, but we had that run and we had that momentum. We had a good team, so it was unfortunate we didn't win it that year

John Caulfield was very good, and he had John Cotter as the assistant manager. I think Billy Woods was in that year as well. We had a good dressing-room. We trained properly and we were a tight group, which is important. The performances on the pitch showed it.

We just didn't get over the line, but we came very close in the first year. It looked like things were going the way they were going to go, that we were getting stronger as a club financially as well with the crowds coming back. The club was going from strength to strength.

You could see it coming and you could see the work that was done in the background with John Caulfield, John Cotter and the board. You could see things happening... better players were coming in and there is no place like Turner's Cross.

When there is 4,000 or 5,000 fans inside there, there is no a better place to play your football. It is a good pitch. I think teams that travel down enjoy playing down there as well. When you are competing and the crowds are in... Turner's Cross is the best place in the country to play your football.

The fans could see what was happening. When the Cork City fans are in and they are behind the team, it can only be a good thing. It drives the team on as well and the players see that. The fans are so important down here.

The senior players were always around to give the younger players advice, if they wanted it. We were always there. Even when I was younger, you looked to the senior players because they have been there and they have done that. I think that is always important, that you have those kind of players in the dressing-room, that young lads can look up to... and if they have any questions or anything like that, they can go and ask you.

It obviously helps financially as well when you are in the Premier Division, it is easier to attract more players. City went on and they won the cup… they won the double. You could see that it was going that way.

The manager and John Cotter, they would look over things, but I probably had the experience of playing in England and I had some very good players in alongside me, such as Gearóid Morrissey and Bucks. A lot of those boys… it was easy to play with.

We had a good work ethic in the middle of the park. We had good wide players and centre-forwards, obviously with Mark O'Sullivan… and then you had Seánie Maguire as we went on. As we put a team together, it was strong through the middle. You had Muzzer (Dan Murray) back there… Benno (Alan Bennett) came in as well, and Kenny Browne. We were very strong.

We lost on the last game of the season up in Dundalk. But the St Pat's game was an important game and one you'll always remember. You could see what we were doing and we were thereabouts at the end of the season. We came up against a very good Dundalk side who had the likes of Pat Hoban, Richie Towell, Daryl Horgan and Stephen O'Donnell.

They pipped us at the end. We had a good side too, and we had good players and we all knew our jobs. We did it, and we were hungry. There was good attitude. It just showed that if you are doing the work off the pitch and on the pitch, you can get results.

Players came away from 2014 with confidence, understanding that we were not far away. With John Caulfield and John Cotter, they could see that as well. They brought in new players and they got rid of a few. The team got stronger and it freshened things up.

For me, I just wanted to play with Cork City, I didn't want to play with anybody else. That is just the way I am… I wanted to play with Cork. When I came back the first time, I had a lot of injuries and it took me a while to get going. It took a few years to get going… I must say.

It is important to have Cork players in the team and we had a few there. When you are playing with your hometown, it means a lot more than to playing with other teams. Cork City has been great for me. I had a lot of serious injuries when I was younger, and I was probably thinking… *will I just pack it all in?*

But I didn't, I came back to Cork and I am very grateful Cork City gave me that opportunity to get my career back on track. I went off signed for Ipswich and I came back. Cork took me back again and I finished my career out.

We won the FAI Cup and it probably was a good time to finish when I was 36. I really enjoyed it.

I am now very privileged to be sitting here as the Cork City FC manager. 2021 was tough and I knew it was going to be tough. It took us a small bit longer than I thought to get going. During the second-half of the season we were up and running, and the confidence was up with a lot of players. But the bad start caught us. Coming towards the end of the 2021 season, however, we were flying.

I know there is a lot of work to be done.

That is the job and that is what we are trying to do. I know it is a building job, but we want to win things as well. We will put in the work and the players will put in the work, I have no doubt about that.

GEARÓID MORRISSEY

KRC GENK 1 ★ CORK CITY 0
UEFA Europa League
Third Qualifying Round First Leg
Luminus Arena
JULY 28, 2016

Gearóid Morrissey in action against Nikolaos Karelis of KRC Genk during the first leg at the Cristal Arena in Genk.

★ **KRC GENK:** M Bizot; S Walsh, S Dewaest, D Wouters, J Uronen, T Buffel, W Ndidi, A Pozuelo, L Bailey, A Samatta, N Karelis. Subs: N Kebano for Kareils, B Heynen for Pozuelo.

★ **CORK CITY:** M McNulty; M McSweeney, A Bennett, K Browne, K O'Connor, G Bolger, S Dooley, G Buckley, **G Morrissey**, S Beattie; S Maguire. Subs: D Morrissey for Beattie, M O'Sullivan for Maguire.

THE ACTION

DESPITE AN EXCELLENT overall performance, Cork City's hopes of UEFA Europa League progression remained in the balance after a narrow defeat at the hands of KRC Genk at Luminus Stadium in Belgium.

John Caulfield's side more than gave a decent account of themselves against a Genk side that went on to reach the quarter-finals of this competition.

City's intent was evidenced early on when Steven Beattie tested the Genk netminder after a fiercely struck effort in the 11th minute. However, it was Genk who took the lead on the half hour mark when the highly rated Leon Bailey planted his effort beyond Cork goalkeeper Mark McNulty.

Genk almost extended their lead through an Ally Samatta effort, which McNulty was on hand to save well. Early into the second-half, City showed further signs of belief that they could get a crucial away goal. A Kevin O'Connor shot was saved well by Genk goalkeeper Marco Bizot, while Seán Maguire had a great chance on the hour mark, when he fired wide from a good position after running impressively into the box.

City continued to look dangerous and lively with Gearóid Morrissey shooting just wide of the mark on 72 minutes after being teed up by Stephen Dooley.

Overall, Cork City were very pleased with the level of their performance. Despite being significant underdogs to win in Belgium over the 90 minutes, City were confident in possession and by no means looked out of their depth.

★★★★★

66

THE ONE THAT really sticks out for me, and where I think we played the best football we have ever played in Cork City shirts, was when we played Genk away in the Europa League qualifiers.

Genk were 10 times the size of us as a club; we had seen their budget before the game and we saw the players we were playing against. I was marking Pozuelo, who was Spanish, played in La Liga and was a serious player. That was just one of their players. They had the likes of Leon Bailey and Samatta. They had a massive squad.

In the first-half, Genk were a bit better than us. But towards the end of the half and in the second-half I thought it was the best football we have ever played in Cork City shirts. It was just pure football and it was actually a pleasure to be involved. I couldn't believe it at the time, we were actually playing them off the park in patches and they obviously would do the same. It was a fantastic game of football.

We ended up losing. Seánie Maguire had a chance and nine times out of 10 he would have scored. Just this particular time, he didn't. That game in Genk epitomised everything about us and everything we were doing.

It just showed us all we were right to have the belief that we had, we were right to think we had a good team with good players. We were playing total football, it was all on the deck. We were playing out from the back. It was the best game of football I ever played I'd say in my life. We ended up losing, I know, but I think that just reassured us… *listen lads, we are a proper football team.*

It didn't suit the narrative that these lads could come together in Cork and, all of a sudden, be top of the league. The fellas up in Dublin wouldn't really be too happy with that. It doesn't suit them when it is not a Dublin team… it doesn't suit them that it is not a Shamrock Rovers that are up the top of the league. The fact was we were beating Rovers 5-0 at that stage, that shows you how far ahead we were and it didn't sit nicely with some people.

That game in Genk, I think that really showed everybody we are not what you are trying to make us out to be at all. We are actually a good footballing team. I think that proved it. We should have come away with a draw. Greg Bolger was in the middle with me and Greg set the tone really because that is how he likes to play, dropping in and getting the ball off the centre-halves and play from there. He kind of set the tone and we all followed suit.

The football we played was fantastic, as I've said. It is one thing I look back on now and I am delighted I was part of it, because it was going toe-to-toe with a team who are regular competitors in the Europa League. It was fantastic that we actually put it up to them. We didn't put it up to them in a way that we parked the bus, we put it up to them and we actually played football.

We were gutted on the bus coming back. Just the feeling in general. We were in one way delighted and then, in the other way as footballers, we were absolutely gutted to be losing out, the fact we thought we deserved something from the game.

We trained the night before the game at the stadium and just looked around at the set-up they had. But it just goes to show there is such a good product here in the League of Ireland, if only someone can channel it properly. If it only got what it just deserves.

John Caulfield was always canvassing for that, that there should be a TV deal. We were almost happy when RTE put us on the TV at all… just delighted that they took an interest.

You can't be operating on a system where you have no TV deal. I think we are the only country in Europe without at TV deal. You have the top three or four teams on 52-week contracts, and then the rest are on 42-week contracts. It beggars belief that you have full-time athletes and, all of a sudden, they are in the dole queue the day after a cup final or the day after the season ends.

What a great league, though. The League of Ireland has given me so much. The memories I have from it are absolutely fantastic and none better than the European memories.

The one thing about John Caulfield, he instilled in all of us a massive belief.

He brought such a belief to the football club. Even in the domestic league, it was Dundalk and St Pat's on top at the time when John first got the job. I remember John straightaway, first thing he was like, 'look, I could be wrong, but I don't think we are that far off them'.

He was like, 'are you telling me that we wouldn't be able to put it up to them on our day!'

He really instilled that belief into us.

We had no right to think that. At the time, we probably would have been lucky to be top of the First Division with the team we had. A year later John added a lot of players. But at that time, with the budget, I'd say if we were top of the First Division we would have taken it.

We ended up starting the season and we drove on. We went into the last game of the season away to Dundalk and all we needed was a draw to win the league. That was down purely to the belief that John had put in us. We had a lot of players from Munster Senior League… we had a lot of young fellas coming in. We had fellas, if probably Cork City were strong, would never have gotten a chance to play with Cork City if the times were good. But it worked out.

All these fellas got a chance and their game came on ten-fold. By the end of the season, they were Cork City players and they were established League of Ireland players and rightfully so. They came up a couple of levels and we were well able, and became well established Cork City players. Going into the next couple of years that followed, that is what happened.

The belief that we had, you couldn't shake us. It didn't matter who we were going to play. We knew what we were good at… we were tough and we were resilient. We were very hard to break down. If you scored a goal against us, you had to work damn hard to get it. But it wasn't just a case of the back four and the goalkeeper.

Everybody got behind the ball as soon as we lost it. Everybody was sprinting back. Then we had quality as well. I don't think that team got enough credit for the quality that we had. Seánie Maguire was without doubt the best player in the country at the time, but you can't forget the other lads who were around the squad.

The quality was unreal. In fairness to John, he signed unbelievably well. The likes of Stephen Dooley! I never heard of Stephen Dooley in my life, and John got him in. I remember the first day of pre-season, and nobody could get near him. His agility was frightening.

We had a lot of quality, and I think that was the difference. We had fellas who were really good players, but there was no egos in our dressing-room. Seánie Maguire was heads and tails above everyone in the league, but you couldn't have met a nicer and more modest lad. John could still give out to him in the dressing-room and he wouldn't say boo back to John. He'd get on with it and we've move on.

That is the mentality that we had, and I think that is what any successful team has. Players are fully behind the manager. They all want the same thing. There was a camaraderie and there was an absolutely solid core, we couldn't really be shaken. John put that together and fair play to him.

The belief John put into us going over there to Belgium, it was just par for the course. We just had that belief and nothing different.

There was a bit more research went into it with John, Lisa Fallon and John Cotter. We had a few more meetings than you would a regular domestic game. To be fair to John, Lisa, Cotts and Biscuits (Phil Harrington), they went into absolute unbelievable detail. We'd even have clips of the referees, and traits of the referees, and how many cards he has been giving out.

Every squad John Caulfield touches he seems to instil that into them, and it is a minimum. It is a minimum of John's teams that they are going to believe in themselves and they are going to work damn hard. The minute John came in, you could see the desire in his eyes. If you sat down with John for 10 minutes, you couldn't help come out of there and feel the exact same way he did.

The passion, the commitment… the belief and the desire, you could tell what he wanted. There was no time for messing about.

He instilled that in each and every one of us and it carried on. It won us the league, it won us cups and it made us competitive in Europe. He doesn't get enough credit for the players he signed… the likes of Stephen Dooley, Jimmy Keohane. People wouldn't have said they were great players at the time… but by the time they left the club everyone knew how good they were.

Seánie Maguire was on the Dundalk bench not getting a run. Nobody knew about him. He came back from England and there wasn't a word said about him around the league, so nobody knew if he was good or bad. John saw glimpses of him and he signed him. Seánie Maguire showed everyone what he already was, which was the best striker in the league and levels above everyone else, destined for England and the international stage. So, John saw that before anyone else had seen it.

That's what happened and John had that about him. I think that is what John was unbelievably good at. John's man-management was good because he didn't miss a trick. He knew what you were doing, what your missus was doing. He knew what you did for the weekend or what the lads did together. He knew what the single lads were up to… he knew the lads that were golfing.

John knew everything about the club and that is what a great manager is… he lives and breathes it. He lives and breathes the players, because they are who win the leagues and cups at the end of the day.

The League of Ireland gets a bad rap. The reality is that any player from England who comes back to the league, they find it difficult to adapt because it is a tough league and it is sprinkled with quality. There is no doubt about it, there are some unbelievable players in the League of Ireland. When players come back from England, if they think they are going to have an easy ride and just pick up a wage packet, the quickly discover it is the complete opposite. They have to be ready for work the same as the rest of us.

We came into training and we were buzzing to come in. Clonakilty were a sponsor of the club in some way and they'd want to come in just to do breakfast mornings with us. The fans wanted to come in and watch training sessions all the time. They wanted to meet the players non-stop. I remember John Caulfield had to filter the interviews that we did, because there was just such a demand.

Éanna Buckley's phone in the office… even our own phones and people getting in contact with us personally. It was non-stop, because we were doing so well. The people of Cork got behind us massively. The likes of SoHo and these places, they just rode in behind us. Whatever we needed and whatever we were doing, they were all just absolutely delighted to have us around them, and to be part of us for a couple of hours. The buzz was fantastic.

Thinking back, it was the time of our life and you don't even realise it… turning up on Grand Parade with the cups, and the reception we got. There are players that go through their whole career and they don't get to win anything or do anything or experience too much. I had some unbelievable years with Cork City. I got to dip my toe into it when we won the First Division in 2011. Then, I got to see the rest of it. I am delighted that I did, and so grateful for it.

It meant everything to be successful at Cork City. I was a lad coming back from England as well. I didn't want to be in England, I was homesick and came home.

Then I was like… *right what do I do now?*

Do I just get a job? Or do I try to make something of the football career that I have put so much time and effort into?

I decided to carry on with football because, in my head, I wanted to succeed.

When I was younger, up to 24 and 25, mid-season breaks meant nothing to me. The older lads, and rightly so, were going on holidays and taking a break, mentally unwinding. I had no interest. I was driving on and I was out in the gym. I was out in Bishopstown practicing. If you are not a young lad doing that, you have no chance.

That is what I would say really. It absolutely killed me to walk away from the club, but I haven't *walked away*. Once you play for Cork City, you are forever a part of it. Once you put on that shirt, and went out and represented the club, I think everybody in the city... they hold you in high esteem.

I am retired and I am still bumping into people. It feels like I am not retired when I get straight into a chat about football. That tells you everything.

JOHN DUNLEAVY

CORK CITY 2 ★ BRAY WANDERERS 1
League Of Ireland Premier Division
Turner's Cross
APRIL 28, 2017

John Dunleavy celebrates after scoring Cork's second goal during the Premier League win over Bray Wanderers at Turner's Cross in 2017.

★ **CORK CITY:** M McNulty; S Beattie, **J Dunleavy**, R Delaney, K O'Connor, C McCormack, G Morrissey, K Sheppard, G Bolger, S Dooley, S Maguire. Subs: J Keohane for Bolger, S Griffin for Dooley, C Ellis for Maguire.

★ **BRAY WANDERERS:** P Cherrie; K Buckley, T Clancy, D Foran, J Marks, J Sullivan, M Salmon, R Brennan, G McCabe, D Connolly, A Greene. Subs: K Moore for Salmon, A Flood for Brennan, J Aherne for McCabe.

THE ACTION

IN FRONT OF over 5,000 supporters at Turner's Cross, Cork City recorded an eleventh straight league victory and moved 12 points clear at the top of the table after this clash with Bray Wanderers.

City showed their attacking intent from the outset, with Karl Sheppard seeing his early effort come back off the post.

The home side were awarded a penalty in the 10th minute, when Bray's Derek Foran was penalised for a jersey tug on Ryan Delaney. Seán Maguire stepped up to take the spot kick and duly converted to the bottom corner for his ninth league goal of the season. The Leesiders had numerous decent chances to add to their advantage in the opening half, including a Stephen Dooley effort which forced a fine save out of Bray 'keeper Peter Cherrie.

Bray started well in the early stages of the second-half, with Gary McCabe shooting just outside the box and Aaron Greene forcing a save out of City goalkeeper Mark McNulty. City however got a second goal in the 87th minute of the game, when Johnny Dunleavy headed in from a Kevin O'Connor corner kick.

Bray got a consolation goal when Derek Foran found the back of the net in second-half stoppage time. But City held on and came away with a victory that saw them keep their one hundred percent winning start.

★★★★★

66

IT WAS JUST the culmination of that goal and that moment, in a big game at Turner's Cross and in front of a big crowd. Having endured what I endured with the injury that I had, which was really horrendous… I did very well to get back playing at all. To come back from that and have a moment like that, in a massive game in front of the Shed, it was just perfect.

It was just a *perfect* moment and one of those that you kind of dream about when you are small, or even when I was out injured. One of the things that keeps you going is the thought of something like that happening. I was lucky enough that it did happen to me. To do it in a big game in front of the Shed, and as captain of Cork City, in a game that went on to help us to win the league… you couldn't write it.

Bray Wanderers were going very well at the time. They came to Turner's Cross and they had a lot of good players. They were actually up near the top along with us, so it was an important game in that season.

I had come back the previous season from one of my bad knee injuries… I had been out for eight or nine months. I came back in and I was playing centre-half against Bray. It was a proper big game and Turner's Cross was rocking… it was brilliant. We went 1-0 up and then with about 10 minutes to go, we got two corners in-a-row. The first corner, I got my head on it and put it towards the goals, but the Bray 'keeper tapped it over.

The very next corner, it came across and I headed it… and it went in. I just remember going and celebrating in front of the Shed.

It is actually my favourite picture ever. I have got the picture up on the wall celebrating that goal.

I remember the feeling of that ball hitting the back of the net… I was almost in tears, just the pure emotion of it, how much it meant to me coming back and scoring in a big game. Captaining Cork City… which I have always said was one of the biggest honours of my life. Everything about that moment was something I will never forget. I get goosebumps even thinking about it now.

I haven't had many feelings like that in football, and I will never forget that night.

The picture, I look at it quite often.

The injury that I had was so serious, you're only maybe 70:30 to play again, maybe even less than that. It had taken a lot of work to even get to that point, but I was playing well at the time and really enjoying my football. I just remember being very comfortable.

We were flying, we were absolutely *flying*.

We were going out every week and it wasn't a case of thinking are we going to win, or can we win, it was more how much are we going to win by. Winning the league, I think it was something that we had to do or we probably would have been a bit unfulfilled. It was brilliant to win the cups and they are phenomenal, but the best team in the league wins the league over the course of a season.

We really had to prove to ourselves nearly as much as anyone else, that we were the best team. The way we started that season, we started like a house on fire. To have one draw out of the league games up to the break, it was phenomenal going. We were pretty much like a train at that point, and it was just a joy to be a part of the team at that time.

The team that we had, there was just some exceptional players… Alan Bennett, who is a total Cork City legend. We were all at a good age and we were close as a group. We really worked hard, and we wanted to win. It was a strong team really.

All these fellas, they were obviously brilliant players, but all these people are really solid people we well. Really good people and boys that you'd love to go out for a drink with or meet again. It wasn't a squad where there was any divide in it or anything like that. As a back four, we didn't concede very much, that's for sure. If somebody was to score past us, they certainly had to work for it.

That was obviously to do with the way we were set up, but also to do with the mentality and the quality of the players that we had. What Seánie Maguire did that year was crazy. He scored so many goals in the first half of the 2017 season that no one in the top scorers' chart could catch him.

It was unreal what he did. The hat-trick that he got in Dundalk the night we beat them 3-0, he really was a machine. You could see it in training and things, he could make people look silly, boys that would be good players… and he would make you look silly. He just had that extra bit of quality. We knew that if ever we were in trouble, he would get us out of it and a couple of times that season he probably did dig us out. It was brilliant to see the success he had going forward.

I was at the game when he made his Ireland debut, myself and Steven Beattie went up to watch him. What a brilliant thing to be able to see, a former teammate of yours making his debut for Ireland.

With the work that Seánie Maguire put in, and coming from where he was coming from to Cork, he deserves everything that he gets… and he's a fantastic fella.

Karl Sheppard was a top League of Ireland player for his whole career. He was a torture for people when he was in Cork and one of those boys you would certainly rather him on your team than against you, that's for sure. He was a seriously good player. Likewise, Stephen Dooley, he was one underestimated footballer… like, *what a player*. He had the lot… pace, power and technical ability. When you have boys like this in your team, even if things aren't going well, a little bit of magic from one of them will pull you out of it. There were plenty of others as well who could pull us out of it.

We were going out every week just full of confidence. We were looking around the dressing-room and thinking… *happy days, no one can beat us*.

But we were very demanding of each other and that tone was set by John Caulfield, John Cotter and the people they had around the club as well. What I always would say about John and likewise with John Cotter, they are both winners. They are winners and they demand very high standards of everyone who works for them and plays for them.

We were no different as a team. The standards were there and we had to hit them. John and John recruited very well as well, along with the rest of the club. The players that were in the squad, there was a real winning mentality there instilled from the top, and there was a real winning mentality in the squad too. John demanded that every week, whether that was in training or matches. It all started in pre-season.

I remember playing a pre-season game up in St Mary's up in the Northside of Cork city. John would have been as demanding that day as he would have been halfway through a season or a big game against Dundalk. He was a brilliant motivator and a brilliant manager. John got the success and that says it all really

There was a real demand placed on us in terms of hard work, and we had to do it well. It fed to us all and we demanded that of each other. I've never played in a team as good as that. It was a pleasure to be part of that dressing-room.

We were going into games just with such confidence, that we were knowing we were going to win. It came to the point that when we beat Dundalk in that game at the break, I think maybe prior to the game we were 15 points ahead of them. People were saying if Dundalk win this they will only be 12 points behind!?!

We went out and we really did put on an exhibition. All of a sudden, we were 18 points ahead going into the break, which was crazy really when you think about it… to be 18 points ahead at the top of a league not even halfway through.

I have always said it, I was so lucky and it was one of the best things I have ever done going down to Cork. I was very lucky in the sense that I was welcomed in pretty much immediately. The people were really good to me and took to me. Hearing a crowd of 5,000, 6,000 or 7,000 people at Turner's Cross and they are singing your name when you are celebrating a win in front of the Shed after a game, there is nowhere like it to play football really. It is a dream of a venue.

It is tight, it is intimidating. When things are going well and the whole lot are behind you, it is fantastic. Those are days you cherish and you wish you could go back, but you can't.

The Cork City supporters would travel everywhere. You could be playing in the Brandywell, a six-hour journey up to Derry… and you would see piles of them there. One of the first games that season we played was against Finn Harps away and it was a horrible night, there was a pitch inspection and everything. It was a significant game for me because I was a Finn Harps fan growing up and I would have gone to watch Harps matches and that.

Here I was captaining Cork City in Finn Park. We won 1-0, but the amount of Cork City fans that had travelled on this horrific night! Look, the Cork City supporters are second to none. There is nowhere like it.

Turner's Cross is tight and it is loud. The people are right behind you and I tell ya, I wouldn't like to be an opposition goalkeeper standing in front of the Shed. I am sure that is not a very pleasant experience. I loved every second of playing in there and especially the big nights when 6,000, 7,000 or 8,000 people were there… the flares are going off and the atmosphere raucous. It was just top class.

It was January 2012 when I signed. Tommy Dunne rang me and asked would I come down to have a look at the club and a look around the place.

At the end of the previous year, I had come down to Cork and I had a cousin living in Cork. So, I rang her and asked, 'could I stay for a night or two, I am going to have a look at Cork City'. I stayed with her anyway and Billy Woods came to pick me up. He showed me around the city and he showed me the training ground.

He showed me Turner's Cross. I remember thinking at the time there was something about it that was just for me. So, I ended up signing and I came down.

I probably didn't realise how big a club it was in the beginning, not until we played a friendly in Youghal. The crowd that was there to watch this pre-season friendly, because we had just been promoted back to the Premier Division... I just couldn't believe it.

The first game we played that year was UCD away and the amount of Cork City fans in UCD that night was just unreal. I got to know very quickly that Cork City is a seriously big football club. I am very thankful that I was taken in so quickly by the Cork City fans and made feel very welcome the whole time I was there. That is something I will always be grateful for.

I have said it before, but I will say it again, it is just a massive, *massive* club. It was a privilege to play with players of the calibre of Mark McNulty, Dan Murray and Colin Healy.

Cork City FC will always be in my heart now because I spent so long there. I was there for seven years and I essentially grew up there in many ways, and became a man at the club. And it meant an awful lot to me to finally get over the line for some trophies.

From my own personal point of view, I'd say especially the league, it meant the world to me. It is a medal I really treasure. To captain Cork City, it was the biggest honour of my career there is no question about it. I remember when John Caulfield mentioned it to me first, I was probably only 23 at the time.

John mentioned that he was thinking of making me captain... and I couldn't believe it. To be captain of a club like Cork City... it was just a total honour and a privilege.

SEÁN MAGUIRE
(& CONOR McCORMACK)

DUNDALK 0 ★ CORK CITY 3
League Of Ireland Premier Division
Oriel Park
JUNE 2, 2017

Seán Maguire, having signed for Preston, celebrates after the FAI Cup final victory over Dundalk at Aviva Stadium in 2017.

★ **DUNDALK:** G Rogers; S Gannon, P Barrett, N Vemmelund, D Massey, C Shields, R Benson, M Duffy, P McEleney, J McGrath, D McMillan. Subs: T Stewart for McGrath, S O'Donnell for Shields, C Kilduff for Duffy.

★ **CORK CITY:** M McNulty; J Dunleavy, A Bennett, R Delaney, K O'Connor, **C McCormack**; K Sheppard, G Morrissey, J Keohane, S Dooley, **S Maguire**. Subs: S Griffin for Dooley, S Beattie for Sheppard, G Bolger for Morrissey

THE ACTION

THIS WAS AN occasion when Cork City made a significant statement of intent in the 2017 League of Ireland Premier Division title race.

A Seán Maguire hat-trick set City on their way to an emphatic victory over Dundalk at Oriel Park, as the Leesiders moved a mammoth 18 points clear at the top of the table and went 17 league games unbeaten in the process.

In the home ground of the champions from the previous season, Maguire put on a masterclass in how to lead the line with his movement and link-up play.

The opening goal of the game arrived in the 18th minute. Stephen Dooley played a neat pass into the path of Karl Sheppard, who crossed for Maguire to sweep the ball home from close range.

The Dundalk progress in the contest was halted on 70 minutes through the clever thinking by City's Johnny Dunleavy, who took a quick throw in off the back of Sheppard, before crossing for Maguire to head beyond the grasp of Gary Rogers.

Maguire, who shortly afterwards signed for English Championship side Preston North End, capitalised on hesitant Dundalk defending to tap into an empty net. Overall, it was a dominant display from Cork City and there was plenty to ponder for Dundalk boss Stephen Kenny, as John Caulfield's side were well on their way to becoming league champions.

★★★★★

66

THE GAME THAT stands out for me is scoring a hat-trick in Oriel Park, and I think for two or three different reasons.

The biggest one was that winning the game basically stamped down that we pretty much had the league won that year. Going up to Oriel... and Dundalk being the team to beat the last couple of years before that. I know we beat them earlier on in that season, but to go up there and to win 3-0!

Personally, I signed a pre-agreement deal with Preston a couple of days before. Then to score three goals up in Oriel Park, to win the game comfortably and then pretty much win the league! And obviously, after having the tough time that I had up there... to score those goals and for the majority of the game getting booed and stuff like that.

I think for me, it is definitely the one game that highlights my time at Cork.

People will look at it and say your most enjoyable game was the 2016 FAI Cup final. But I probably would have said the opposite about the cup final because I had an absolute stinker for the whole game, and probably the only thing I did right was putting the ball in the back of the net. I think of this Dundalk game because it was an important game in Oriel, whereas the year before we lost 2-1 and we pretty much lost the league.

So, I felt I just had that anger and disappointment going up there, going... *we are not letting this happen again... we are not letting Dundalk get back into the league... and we are going to put the league to bed.*

It is the one for me that will live long in the memory.

Thankfully, we did that, because nearly every bit of emotion just showed that day. Obviously scoring a hat-trick just topped it all off. I felt while I was at Dundalk I didn't really get to show anyone the player I was really, because I just didn't get a chance and I didn't get a fair crack at the whip from a playing perspective.

I felt that going to Cork, that I wanted to prove a few people wrong... or, to be fair, a lot of people wrong.

I just had that motivation, that drive to do so. That is the one that probably meant the most to me, and probably in my career to date those are the goals that mean the most to me, to be quite honest. The year previously when we went toe-to-toe, we lost out on the league. I remember playing that game up in Oriel when we lost 2-1.

Daryl Horgan scored for Dundalk and Mark O'Sullivan came on for us and scored. I think we felt at that time that was the one we let slip away. I didn't want to feel like that again.

We ended the season strongly by winning the cup. But obviously the following year we did the double.

For the first goal, Shep (Karl Sheppard) put it across and I scored. I ran around the goal and I remember I was getting pure abuse from the Dundalk fans. At some stage a few of them threw stuff at me, and threw water all over me, something like that.

It just made me feel good, and actually it made me just want to kick on and score more. We were going into every game feeling that we were going to beat whoever was in front of us.

Every single one of us was just full of confidence, and literally everyone was chipping in with goals. We were playing really good football at the time. Thankfully, it showed with the scoreline that day… it showed how far ahead we were!

Everyone was just enjoying our football, and because we had pretty much the same team every week, we were a little bit telepathic in a way… where we knew what runs to make and the runs our teammates were going to make. It was me, Karl Sheppard and Stephen Dooley up front and I thought we were a force to be reckoned with.

I thought we were the three best forwards in the league that year.

Then you had Greg Bolger, Badge (Conor McCormack) vying for that No 6 role… Chops (Gearóid Morrissey), Bucks (Garry Buckley), Jimmy Keohane, who goes under the radar for that year. I thought he was unbelievable. The back four speaks for itself and then we had Nults (Mark McNulty) in goals. Everyone just gelled together.

That team, that year, will probably will go down in League of Ireland history, for how long we stayed unbeaten and how many games we won in-a-row.

One thing that stands out for me is when I joined the club. Meeting up with John Caulfield, we were talking, and he said if you win a trophy and a league in Cork, you'd always be remembered. From literally walking to the shop or walking in to get a haircut, you'll always be remembered and get stopped by every second person.

What he said, literally, came true. During that period, even going in meeting the boys for coffee and stuff like that, we'd be hounded. It was just a great buzz around the place. The club didn't win the league in 12 years. We had just won the FAI Cup the year before, so we felt like we really needed to kick on. I think that was probably at a time where I was really at my peak and enjoying football, to be quite honest… that four- or five-month period where we won 12 or 13 games in-a-row. But honestly, just the buzz around the place and living in the place!

Going to training and going to games, it felt that like you couldn't get a seat going to Turner's Cross no matter who we played.

I probably owe everything to John Caulfield, to be honest. I know, obviously, he will say differently and that I had to do it on the pitch. But I will say otherwise.

I met John at one of the service stations on the road from Cork to Dublin, near Kilkenny. One of the things that stands out was when he said, 'if you win the league in Cork you will be remembered for a long time!'

Another one was when he said, 'look Seánie, I will be giving you a chance, it is up to you if you want to take it or not'.

I will never forget that conversation and I think it was a relationship that just took off straightaway. From that moment, John saw a little bit of me in him. John scored a lot of goals and is a Cork City legend.

Even little tips off him, whether it's in training or in games, stuff like that we just trusted each other straightaway. That is what made the relationship work so well.

I say about John, literally, I probably owe everything to him. I wanted somebody to give a little trust in me, and trust me in playing and turning my career around. He did that, he gave me the chance and I took it.

To this day, I still keep in contact with him all of the time. If I had one person that I would say had the biggest impact on my career from a sporting perspective, it would definitely be John Caulfield.

I felt that the partnership that Karl Sheppard, me and Stephen Dooley had was probably up there with the best front three in the last 10 years in the League of Ireland. The three of us were slightly different in many ways.

In a one vs one scenario, Dools with his trickery and with his skill, I think he was frightening at times. He used to light up Turner's Cross in some games. Shep used to be so direct. He used to get at defenders and get balls into the box. The three of us scored a lot of goals between us. I think that is why it worked so well.

It was anything that I touched felt like it was going to be a goal. I didn't have to think about it twice, it was just instinct… BANG, BANG! I'd be going into games thinking… *I'll be disappointed if I only get one.* I think it is a good thing to be thinking that. At the end of the day, it is all about winning games no matter how you play. But I was going into games thinking… *I know am going to score today… I know I will get a chance.*

I felt kind of loved at Cork City, inside and outside of football. I loved living there, so it is kind of like a home away from home. Obviously, I grew up in Kilkenny a couple of hours up the road. But if I ever move back to Ireland, I think I would be moving back to Cork. Even when I go back on weekends now, anytime I get a chance I'll be straight into Turner's Cross.

When I am back and when I do get the opportunity, I will be going down. Even when I retire, I am a fan for life basically. I think even before I signed with the club, I knew it was the biggest club in Ireland. At Turner's Cross it was averaging around 3,000 or 4,000, I don't think you'd get that anywhere else. Then on the big game nights at Turner's Cross, you were getting a good 6,000 or 7,000.

Even to this day, when I go back to Cork, there are supporters and people who go to games and they still come up chatting or whatever. It is a proud feeling for my family, who are only living a couple of hours up the road. They used to buzz coming down to Turner's Cross every second Friday.

Even the times where I used to come out of the changing room, and the games would be over at 9:30pm, but I wouldn't get home until 11pm or 11.30 pm, because I'd be standing outside signing autographs, signing jerseys for kids and talking to everyone. I loved every second of it.

I know I have made international caps for Ireland. Making your debut and scoring your first goal for Ireland, they are the standouts. Going to Preston… I am now at Preston coming up to five years. I have loved my time at Preston and am loving it at the moment.

But I think my time at Cork City was the pinnacle in terms of happiness and that is where I want to be. That is what I would tell anyone. I have had a lot of highs at Preston, and even before I joined Cork, I had a few highs in schoolboy football and going over to West Ham. I'd probably be lying if I said otherwise, in terms of that bit of enjoyment. Cork City was where I was scoring all of my goals… we won a league title, and we won a cup.

It was probably the best time of my life, to be quite honest, that year and a half… outside of football, family, and friends happy. I met Claudia at the time, and we got married in the summer of 2022. In football, the first year I ended up top goalscorer and won Young Player of the Year. In the same year winning the cup. The next year, I won top goalscorer and won Player of the Year. Then we ended up winning the league and I got a dream move back to England, which is what I always wanted.

I am a fan now when I am away from the club. I have been looking up every scoreline since I left. I feel like they are not too far away. They will get back to where they were in terms of when we were there and what we were doing, it just needs a bit of time.

There is no better man to do that than Colin Healy. There is a young team in there at the moment, but it is only a matter of time. The club isn't too far away from kicking on.

CONOR McCORMACK

Conor McCormack (left) and Karl Sheppard celebrate following the FAI Cup final against Dundalk in 2017.

"

WE JUST KNEW going up there that we were a good few points ahead. But Dundalk were coming back into their stride and they thought then if they beat us, that would close the gap and might throw us off our tracks. We knew it was going to be a massive game.

We went up there obviously to win the game. We set out, and John had his tactics done perfectly. I expected Dundalk to come out all guns blazing, which they did. But we easily put the stamp on them then and put out their fires, nullifying their best attacking threats. Any chance Seánie Maguire was going to get or any of our forwards, we knew we could score at any minute of any game with the quality of forward players that we had.

It was a matter of just keeping it tight at the back, which we did perfectly and

Seánie did the business in the box. He tore their defenders apart.

They were good experienced players who had won numerous leagues, and he still managed to tear them apart. I think everything on the day worked out perfectly, like we had imagined. John Caulfield has to take a massive bit of credit for that because he had us set up perfectly. Going up there, keeping a clean sheet and going 18 points clear of them at the mid-season break and scoring three goals… you couldn't have written it any better.

We were just delighted for that and, thankfully, it happened and it worked out.

Seánie Maguire getting the first goal was brilliant. I think as a team, nobody could have touched us that day. I wouldn't say there is one standout moment, but as soon as we got the third goal, we knew we weren't going to get beaten. To be honest, when I was playing against Seánie, I thought he was a good player. I was at Derry City before that and I don't think he scored against us… and we played Cork three or four times in that spell. We knew he was a dangerous player.

It was only when I went down to Cork that I realised how good he was in training. I think he just went to a new level that year in 2017 and the guys would say that themselves. He was a good player and scoring goals before that, but he was just exceptional when he came back for pre-season and in training you couldn't get near him. You couldn't get the ball off him, he was so strong and quick and powerful.

A great finisher.

I certainly didn't know how good he was until I was actually playing with him and each day training with him. He deserved his chance and I am glad he has gone over and taken it.

It was great to go and beat Dundalk in their own backyard. The fans that travelled up; I am sure they had a good day and a night out of it as well. At the final whistle, when you win 3-0 away at Oriel Park… there are not many teams do that. It was a proud moment for me obviously.

All of my family was there, my close family there supporting me… my cousins and uncles support Dundalk. I had the upper-hand then through the slagging battles over them years.

We knew in ourselves that we had a great team and we even had a great squad. The bench was just as strong as the first eleven, you could have put anybody on. We were all fighting for our place and training was so intense.

We went up and we knew that we could beat Dundalk.

We knew it was going to be tight. But we literally just blitzed them completely and I think it knocked the stuffing out of them then. It was really a statement of intent and I think it opened everyone's eyes towards the league, that it was going to be Cork City's year and thankfully it was.

You are not a proper footballer if you don't look forward to the big games. Especially top of the table and cup final clashes… they were great games to play in. When you want to win as many of them as you can, it usually gives you the upper-hand. Whoever wins the most times against each other usually wins the league.

I don't think any of the other teams were even close to the two clubs at the time.

As a player, definitely you relish playing against the best players in the league and the big games. Certainly, I did anyway and I think my performances improved when I played against the better teams. They were really enjoyable because Dundalk had some fantastic players who won a lot of trophies. Especially for me playing in the middle, playing against the likes of Stephen O'Donnell and Patrick McEleney, those sort of guys were brilliant players. I played with Patrick up in Derry before.

I did enjoy the big games against him because he is a big, powerful, strong guy. I just used to get in nice and tight to him and nibble the ball off him all of the time, frustrate him. If you can nullify their best players in the game, it gives you a chance, especially when we had the likes of Karl Sheppard, Stephen Dooley, Kieran Sadlier and Maguire up top… Garry Buckley at the time was on fire.

If you gave them half a chance in and around the box, they were scoring goals.

It was my job to stop the fires in the middle of the park… covering back if someone was out of position. It was up to me to read space or read where the ball could land. I think I have done that over the years. That is one of my strengths off the ball I think… to be in the right place at the right time.

We had good leaders in the team. I think everyone acted as a captain, to be honest. Everyone was strong and everyone wasn't afraid to let their voices be heard. If you were not putting the work in, guys were on your case. It wasn't acceptable to *not* turn up.

John Caulfield implanted that into us early on. That we knew we weren't going to have any passengers on our team and everyone had to work their socks off. We had plenty of players even to come off the bench to introduce a bit of energy towards the end of the game, shut games out… or if we were looking for a goal.

When we were going into those games, even if it was 0-0 right until the end, we knew we were going to get chances because we had the quality players and we were just going to break teams down. Teams found it very difficult to keep us out. We were just bombarding them constantly until we got those sort of goals. Right from the back, from Mark McNulty right up the pitch, you had the likes of Gearóid Morrissey, Steven Beattie… these types of guys and characters.

We certainly had a lot of big characters who really stood up in the big games and the big moments. They were fantastic players. At the minute, these have still been the best moments of my footballing career. I really enjoyed it and I couldn't have asked for it to have gone any better.

Starting off in 2017, it was just brilliant… and 2018 was still a really good season, we were unfortunate we got beaten in a cup final and we finished second to Dundalk. Then, in 2019 it was a pity the way it went and the way the club kind of fell a little bit. Everyone who played there really wanted to be there.

We lost a lot of good players in those couple of years who went away to England or other clubs. Then we found out about the financial situation, which was hard to take because a lot of us really liked being down in Cork and playing for Cork City.

It was a pity the way it went. Going from the success we had from 2017… if you had said I was going to be there and I was going to win the double and become the club captain, I would have snapped your hand off. I really enjoyed it and it will definitely always be in my heart.

We are still all good mates. We all still have WhatsApp groups together. My best mates still would be Karl Sheppard and Steven Beattie from the team. We still have kept in touch with each other and we meet up as much as we can. We always call each other at the weekends. They will be friends forever and I am really privileged to have been part of that. I loved every minute of it.

Throughout the whole squad, we were a good bunch of lads. We can look at each other and say we gave everything… and, thankfully, it paid off.

John Caulfield is probably one of the best managers in the League of Ireland, I believe, certainly since I have come into the league anyway. He has won numerous trophies as a player and now as a manager. He is a Cork City man through and through. Everything he wanted was for the best interests of the club and for the people and the supporters.

He made sure that we knew that in teams meetings, that everything was for the club, for the city and for Cork in general. He really demanded that from us and pushed us to our limits. He made sure we got the best out of each other. But we all respected each other and whatever happened on the training pitch you forget about it, and moved onto the next day

If someone had an argument over a tackle, you just got up and shook hands and you got on with it then. There were no clicks or little side groups in the dressing-room. He was so determined and treated everyone with respect. I think that is why he is such a great manager. He is certainly a great man-manager as well. If you had any problems off the field, he would help you out. He really is a top manager and one of the best I have ever played for.

I knew that Cork City were a big club and they had their problems years before that. When I first came into the league, they were in the First Division. They eventually got themselves back into the Premier Division. We played them a few times when I was with St Patrick's Athletic, Shamrock Rovers… at the time playing against them.

I always enjoyed games going down to Turner's Cross. I knew it was going to be hard. There was nearly like a hostile environment going down there because they are so passionate and believe in their team so much. They wanted the team to win so much. Certainly, you knew going down that you were going to get a tough game, that you were never going to get the points very easily.

Once you are actually playing for Cork City, they are cheering you on and pushing you on right until the last minute… they are actual like being the 12th man.

Shooting into the Shed end, it gives you the extra boost as well. So, I knew how big it was, but only when I actually joined there… then I realised it is a huge, *huge* club and probably one of the best in Ireland. I am very fortunate that I got a chance to play for them and I loved every minute of it.

Cork City were very close a couple of times and just fell short towards the end. They lost one on the last day of the season in 2014 up in Oriel Park and so the lads were obviously very disappointed with that, and John was as well. But John built a team and he built a squad that was really going to push Dundalk and eventually turn them over.

The Cork City fans are very welcoming. I still get a couple of messages throughout the year from Cork City fans, wishing me luck and all the best, and if I am ever down to give them a shout. Even now, when I am playing against them, after the games or before the games, the fans will always clap me off.

There is definitely respect there and there is definitely respect there for me back towards the club. Without them, I wouldn't have won the double. I still have an apartment down in Cork, so I feel there is a bit of me that will always be down there. They are great people.

STEVEN BEATTIE

CORK CITY 0 ★ DERRY CITY 0
League Of Ireland Premier Division
Turner's Cross
OCTOBER 17, 2017

Steven Beattie scores at Turner's Cross.

★ **CORK CITY:** M McNulty; **S Beattie**, A Bennett, R Delaney, S Griffin, C McCormack, G Morrissey, J Keohane, G Buckley, S Dooley, K Sheppard. Subs: K Sadlier for Dooley, C McCarthy for Beattie, A Campion for Sheppard.

★ **DERRY CITY:** G Doherty; C McDermott, A Barry, D Cole, D Jarvis, H Monaghan, A McEniff, B Doherty, B McNamee, R Curtis, R Patterson. Sub: N Low for Jarvis.

THE ACTION

A HOME DRAW against Derry City saw the League Of Ireland Premier Division title return to Cork City for the first time in 12 years.

John Caulfield's side needed just a single point to land the club's third ever league title and their first since 2005. It took the home side 26 minutes to finally have their first sight of goal but Gearóid Morrissey's ambitious strike from distance drifted over the Derry goal.

Derry almost grabbed a sensational opener through Rory Patterson after half an hour played.

In the second-half, the atmosphere grew tense as Cork were unsure whether to settle for the point that would seal the title or go in search of the winner and clinch it in style.

In the end, it was the former as Cork kept control of possession, refused to take any chances going forward and sealed league title glory.

John Caulfield was a league winner with Cork City as a player and on this particular night he became one as a manager as well.

★★★★★

❝

STORM OPHELIA KNOCKED down the stadium. We could have won it the week before against Dundalk. We were so far clear, but the storm hit and then I am thinking… *here, we are never going to win this thing.*

We found out two days before that the game was going to go ahead. I think the game was on a Tuesday night. For health and safety reasons, the Derrynane Stand was gone, so we ended up winning it with three-quarters of our stadium full, when otherwise it would have been packed.

The blood, sweat and tears that went into it… not just that year, but also the disappointment of 2016… and '15, finishing second and being a bridesmaid to Dundalk. There was just pure relief that we had finally done it. After so many years when the club had not won a league, suddenly, you are a part of history.

No matter if you played for just five minutes of the year or started in every game, you are after making history for a football club that you really, *really* love. So, it was just an outburst of everything. I remember the dressing-room afterwards… the tunnel, the fans coming out onto the pitch.

My uncle played for Shelbourne and Shamrock Rovers for years and he won so many leagues. He used to tell me the first one you will never forget. I have seen videos of when he won… and then for me to be standing there, lads coming up to you and grown men crying, it was unbelievable to be fair.

I don't have kids, so I can probably say it is the best moment of my life. When I finally have kids, I'd say I might change that, but at the moment it was the best feeling ever to be honest with you.

We lost Seánie Maguire halfway through that year and we didn't really replace him with an out and out goalscorer. So straightaway, you're missing out on goals. We still had the quality players, but we just weren't scoring goals. Then you see the media giving us a bit of stick, saying things like we are a one-man team. We took a lot of offence to that because we put Seánie into positions to score the goals.

I know he is an unbelievable player and one of the best I have ever played with, but they forget that there was 10 lads behind to help him get where he went. Then, suddenly, we are supposedly a crap team because one player has left.

Before the Derry game, I think we said that it is a pain in my arse listening to this s****e, so that was kind of the added incentive. We'd always wanted to win it at home as well. I think we were away after the Derry game to Pat's that weekend. When you're winning the league, you'd win it up in Finn Harps on a Tuesday, wet and windy night, if necessary!

But if you could pick, it would obviously be at home. So, we said before the Derry game, that we are running out of opportunities to win it at home. We said the Cork City fans deserved to be there, in their home and church in Turner's Cross. You always want to win it at home… in front of your fans and your people. These people who stuck through with the club when it was on its knees… FORAS being set up and people putting money out of their own pockets to save the club.

I heard all the stories, such as how they literally had to throw a team together in the First Division for a trip to Derry. So, for those people, to do it in Cork… it just meant so much to a lot of people. If it was an away game, people mightn't have been able to be there for whatever reason. To win the title in Turner's Cross was special. It is a night which I will not forget. People still remind me of that night, grown men and young men. So, I know it meant a lot. I think it is not until you go into the dressing-room and you are just with the players and management, that it sinks in that you have finally won the league. You've sacrificed… even me, moving my life down here to Cork. I never really went home to Dublin, and it took two and a half years to finally get to where I wanted to be… to win the league.

I wanted to win a league down here and to be successful. Then you are thinking about all of the sacrifices you've made with regards to family, and personal life.

We won the cup in 2016 in the Aviva, and that was my first silverware ever professionally. Then you get a taste of winning the league and the outburst of emotion from the fans, because that was our target all year. Suddenly, you have another target and a chance to make even more history.

You are not happy just to win the league, you want to win everything. We were saying all week… *think about it, we are going to be heroes if we win this.*

We'll be known forever as the team that won the double.

In extra-time we went one down and that mentality kicks in, that we are not going to lose this game. We got a goal back and that is just how it was. We were just psychopaths to win the games. The main strength one hundred percent was the strength of the dressing-room. I mean it was rock solid and water-tight.

Anything that happened in that dressing-room stayed in that dressing-room.

Nothing was ever leaked. Lads would have been p****d off if they were not playing, but they'd still walk around and shake everyone's hand and wish them the best of luck. Training was an unbelievable standard. Everyone wanted to play because we were doing so well. The strength in depth of the team... if I wasn't playing, I knew someone else could come in and do an equal if not better job. That was across the team.

We strengthened mid-season and got Kieran Sadlier. To see the likes of Sadlier not starting games... Karl Sheppard or Stephen Dooley, you are like... *this is a good team.* So it was definitely the strength and, from my perspective, with Nults behind me and the back four... it was probably one of the best back fours I ever played in. You had Kevin O'Connor left back, me right back. At centre-back... Alan Bennett and Ryan Delaney, who was on loan at the time.

Even the year before that, we had Kenny Browne in there instead of Delaney. We had just some unbelievable players. Once we kept a clean sheet, we knew we were going to win the game because we were so good going forward. Just give the ball to Maguire, give the ball to Dooley or Sheppard... Gearóid or Garry Buckley and leave them to do their magic, while we keep it tight at the back.

From my perspective it was an easy job for me, really. But just how tight the group was, made it a special, *special* group.

I knew how big the club was from playing against Cork. I played down in Turner's Cross for Bohs, and for Sligo against Cork. I used to up my game so much just because it was in Cork. The fans were on your case and giving you stick, but I loved it. I always said I'd love to play down here because you see how packed Turner's Cross is and how passionate the Cork City fans are.

When I signed for City in the transfer window in 2015, the first couple of days with social media and stuff, I was like... *this is a big deal down here.*

There was added pressure when you are coming from Dublin.

You have to hit the ground running and deliver because, let's be honest, the Dubs would probably get the blame first. But that was the pressure I wanted. I scored on my debut and that just triggered my career at City and I just didn't look back. I have loved every second of it.

You see old men who have been going to Turner's Cross for years and have a chat with them after the game, the likes of Jerry Harris around the club, and the likes of John Kennedy who passed away... people who ate, slept and breathed the club. They just love Cork City and that filters into the players, no matter where you are from. You go out on a Friday night not minding letting yourself down, you don't want to let those people down because it will actually ruin their week.

It is definitely a unique club in that sense, and you can feel the community side of it. We have lost fans throughout the years since I first came to Cork and it leaves a void. Not just around the city, but within the club and within the lads that have been here because you know these faces from Turner's Cross over the years.

Then to see them pass away, it just brings it all home how tight and close this football club is.

They were great days and, looking back, you nearly took them for granted. Especially in 2017, you were nearly going out thinking how many goals are you going to win the game by. My biggest advice for anyone is if they are ever going to be in that position again, don't take it for granted. When you are in it, you think it is going to last forever. You are like... *we will be unbelievable again next year and we will be brilliant the following year.*

Myself and John Caulfield had the biggest love-hate relationship in the world.

I don't think people even know about how love-hate it was. I love the man and I know he loves me, but we also had some arguments and that is John's biggest strength. I said it to him in his office a couple of times, 'you should be a politician, not a football manager'.

You'd go there on a Monday morning, say if he dropped you on Friday and you were fuming all weekend, thinking... *right, I am going to say this!*

So, you knock on the door and he'd be like, 'tit down there Beatts, alright'. He would start chatting with you, just about life, how is your missus… and how is your family. That'd put you in a good mood then, and you forget what you were going to say to him. You were going in p****d off that you were not playing. His player-management was brilliant. If John needed to batter you, he would batter you… if he needed to put an arm around you, he would put an arm around you.

What I loved about John, and it was probably mine and his biggest flaw, was that we were so passionate, and that's why we sometimes clashed. As you look back on it now, we both wanted the same thing. But we were so enthusiastic and passionate about it. We could clash on the training ground… like bad, and then the next morning it was just normal.

It was not like a father-son relationship, but it was like we are onto the next day of training we cannot waste it. That's how we were. Lads will tell you the more you talk about that year, how we clashed. I think he played games with you, where he didn't play me for three or four weeks for no reason at all.

I was training well and playing well, and he took me off at half-time in one game. Then, I didn't play for three weeks and I was like... *my head is gone here.* Then he would make me captain for the next game. I was like... *what is going on here? I am not playing one week and now I am captain.*

I cannot speak any more highly of John Caulfield, though. He could get every player in the dressing-room to run through a wall for him and buy into what he is doing. I think he was a massive part of how tight-knit that dressing-room was. It was rock solid.

John was loyal to us and we were loyal to John. There was no bullshit with us.

If you went to our training ground, you would be like... *these lads hate each other.* But that is just the way we were. We were so close off the pitch, and in the build-up to training. Once you crossed that training pitch, you were like... *I want to start this week, Gearóid Morrissey wants to start in the eight position or Greg Bolger wants to play in the six.*

That was another Caulfield strength, he just knew when the boiling point was too much, but he would let it simmer. Honestly, the lads would tell you, I had fist fights with Greg Bolger in training, we went head-to-head in training. I went head-to-head with Bucks (Garry Buckley), different lads went head-to-head. It would happen. Then, you'd shake hands afterwards and go for a coffee.

So, when you are talking about strong mentality… these were training games, where you'd lose a five-a-side and we were ripping into someone.

If someone gave you a bad pass, you are ripping into them. But you are mates and that is just how it was. It is a testament to the squad that John put together.

John told me for years that when he goes to look at new players, he knows they can play but he literally goes to meet them three or four times. He finds out about their parents and friends. John wants people that can fit into the mould of the group as a person, literally, before a player.

He knows what they can do as a player, but he won't bring them in if they don't fit the group. John used to ask us about players we'd know in the League of Ireland. If something happened in that dressing-room, he'd go and find out and wouldn't even sign them. That is just how he kept it tight, tight… *tight.*

John was also great. If we had three or four hard weeks, he'd say, 'lads, go and have a team night out Saturday night because you are off on Sunday'. Everyone went out together. That was another one of John's strengths… he'd see when he needed to step in. Say if we were playing in Europe and you'd fly home on the Friday and have a game on the Sunday, he'd see you were tired and go, 'lads, enjoy yourselves and have a night out'.

He'd put a few quid behind the bar.

That was massive because it would get everyone out and, for one night, you are not talking about football. You are having a bit of craic with the lads. That was another testament to John Caulfield and John Cotter, Mick Punch and Liam Kearney, all the staff in there. They had a great knack of identifying when they needed to step in.

Training would finish and you'd be buzzing to get in for training the next day, wanting to train and wanting to play games. The majority of the group was just loving football and just loving life.

Cork City has been the most enjoyable part of my playing career by a long stretch, and the best of times, not just in my football but in my life. I just loved the group of lads.

ACHILLE CAMPION
(& KARL SHEPPARD)

CORK CITY 1 ★ DUNDALK 1
(After extra time, Cork City win 5-3 penalties)
2017 FAI Cup Final
Aviva Stadium
NOVEMBER 5, 2017

Achille Campion shoots to score the first goal during the FAI Cup final between against Dundalk in 2017.

★ **CORK CITY:** M McNulty; S Beattie, A Bennett, R Delaney, S Griffin, C McCormack, G Morrissey, J Keohane, G Buckley, S Dooley, **K Sheppard**. Subs: K Sadlier for Keohane, G Bolger for Morrissey, **A Campion** for Buckley.

★ **DUNDALK:** G Rogers; S Gannon, B Gartland, N Vemmelund, D Massey, S O'Donnell, R Benson, J McGrath, P McEleney, M Duffy, D McMillan. Subs: D Connolly for McGrath, S Hoare for Gartland, J Mountney for McEleney.

THE ACTION

CORK CITY FC secured a historic league and cup double following a dramatic FAI Cup decider against Dundalk that went all the way to a penalty shootout at the Aviva Stadium.

After a tense contest had finished scoreless after 90 minutes, extra-time was needed to determine the victors just like in the 2015 and '16 cup finals between these pair of teams.

Dundalk went into the lead courtesy of Danish defender Niclas Vemmelund in the fifth minute of extra-time, who was on hand to head into the back of the net from a Michael Duffy free kick.

In the 111th minute of play, City got back on level terms. Getting onto a neat pass from Karl Sheppard, Achille Campion controlled the ball well by chesting it down, before volleying low to the left corner beyond the grasp of Dundalk goalkeeper Gary Rogers.

That sent the contest into a penalty shootout. Karl Sheppard, Greg Bolger, Conor McCormack and Steven Beattie of Cork City – along with David McMillan, Stephen O'Donnell and Robbie Benson of Dundalk – all converted their spot kicks. City goalkeeper Mark McNulty proved to be the shootout hero, successfully saving Duffy's spot kick.

Kieran Sadlier then stepped up and he buried the spot kick away to clinch FAI Cup glory for the Leesiders. A dramatic end to the most memorable of campaigns for Cork City.

★★★★★

"

TO ME, IT is obviously the FAI Cup final, because it concluded the season for all of us as a group. That year, there was a real team spirit, that's actually rare in most football clubs. Even though you are playing team sports, it is a rare thing to all be looking for one goal and to make the scarifies necessary towards that goal.

To me, it is not even the personal aspect of that final that matters, it is the accomplishment.

At the beginning of the season John Caulfield made clear all the objectives of the team. It was an amazing feeling to cross them one by one, just like a 'to do' list. You just cross them one by one all together and everyone reaches their goal, it just feels like almost a machine.

The goal in the cup final for me was a very, *very good* feeling because I was very frustrated with not playing. I literally warmed up for 40 minutes. I had trained previously and I had trained a month, with my mindset on scoring in the final… and I needed to score in the final. Everything, my whole training, was based towards that.

To be there doing side to sides on the sideline was very frustrating. But the opportunity to come on… it is amazing. How it humbles you not to have the opportunity. Then, afterwards, to come in and to respect that opportunity, to give it everything for your team. When you come onto the pitch, you almost feel like you are being unleashed and you are ready for the occasion.

I remember coming on with Greg Bolger as well. Which definitely helps, because he is a tremendous player. It was an incredible feeling. The feedback that I got from the fans looking up at the stand, a full stand of Cork City fans was unbelievable. It was the first time I almost get slapped across the face, just by the emotion that was given to me from the fans. You think you give pleasure to people as a player.

But, oh my God… what I received on that day, just the little 10 seconds where the Cork City fans were going crazy. It was an unbelievable emotion that I have never lived before and since.

If you look on paper at every position, we nearly had the best player in the league in every position. In the camp we knew that. Even if you look at a lad like Connor

Ellis. He was a young lad coming through and if you even look at his stats from that season, he had done fantastically well.

If you look at every single position… you look and we had Greg Bolger on the bench for the FAI Cup final, how crazy is that? I think we knew we were highly capable of doing it. Having won the league previously, which was an amazing league win, it was filling us with confidence. The coaching staff prepared fantastically well and we knew the Dundalk team by heart.

Mark McNulty literally knew every penalty taker from the other team and what they were going to do beforehand. So, it is straightforward, you are just playing on statistics if the guy is gonna do what he does usually, you have a good chance of winning.

I think we lived up to the event. I rewatched the game not too long ago. Everybody was level-headed and fighting for each other. We kept focused the whole time. The game was never over, even when Dundalk scored. We knew that we could come back easily. If you watched even after I scored, I felt like the team knew that we could probably win it before the penalties.

It was fantastic and they are the type of games that define a career. For me, what was very nice was that I didn't have the best season in 2017, even though I was coming off a positive career path. I then made up for my lack of play. It was crazy how just one goal makes up for your lack of play. That is how big the event is.

I was one hundred percent keen to make a mark. You are a professional player. You have a chance given to you. There is no two ways about it and, to be fair, the way that I had been welcomed by the staff, the club and the players, I felt like I was from Cork when I came on.

I didn't even feel French or whatever, I felt like I was from Cork and I am going to win for Cork, no one is stopping me. It was a very pleasant game to be a part of. I felt like that year the final lacked a bit of promotion from the FAI, if I may say. But Mark McNulty took care of promoting the game alright.

But it is a rivalry and to me on that night, it showed how much heart the Cork City fans have because they never doubted during the game. I think the previous games were close games every time. To keep believing until the end shows the character of the fans.

At Sligo Rovers, I was doing very well. I was in negotiations with Sligo and I didn't know too much about Cork City, apart from that they were the toughest team I played, during the end of the season with Sligo.

They were by far the toughest. The defenders… they had Alan Bennett and Kenny Browne. I was like… *oh my God, those are some tough, tough boys.* The way they were playing and smooth, it was educated football. In Ireland there's a few really good players. A lot of people say Ireland is just like England and they lump the ball. But that is not always the case. The likes of Greg Bolger, when I saw that, I was… *this is football.*

I played at Turner's Cross with Sligo during that stint as well, and I loved it. It was really nice. I don't have an extensive experience of the fanbase in Ireland. All I know is from my career path. I arrived from England to Sligo and they took really good care of me there. I honestly feel there are some similarities between the Sligo fans and the Cork City fans. They are a bit isolated from the rest of the country, if I may say. My career was doing good and I had good support from the fans.

So, to find the similar support in Cork was unbelievable. When I arrived, I was supposed to replace Seánie Maguire… and Seánie never left that year, he stayed. It was a bit frustrating, but Seánie was banging the goals in so there was no reason for change. Even then, the support from the fans was massive for me.

It is no news to anyone that Cork City is not a plastic club, it is real fans. It is a family club, but it has a broader reach than just a family club and that is amazing about it.

I still talk to some fans and there is no problem. If tomorrow I go back to Cork, I have a good time with everybody. They also know I gave my everything to the club. So, I feel like Cork City fans, as long as you give one hundred percent, they will give you your credit.

The standard was incredible. The willingness to win everything, what I mean is… every little game and warm-ups were out of this world. I've rarely seen anything like it. People gave it everything for every little detail. When you are preparing for such a big event and you already know everybody is doing all of the little things right, you can only have confidence.

A lot of people didn't wish us well, whether it be a newspaper from Dublin or fans of other clubs that didn't wish us well at all. That fuelled us.

I think if you look at the team, over a period of time there were a lot of players that were in the group and they were the core of the group. Every little addition was integrated and some were integrated and it was a success, some weren't. I think the club was really smart at that time into their additions. To me, I didn't do the best integration into the group at the beginning because I was a bit cocky, and I was very confident in my level of play.

So, then I sucked it up, worked very hard… and the respect came both ways.

They saw I wouldn't just cruise along. I was willing to work and do the dirty work. Even if it is not pretty, but it makes the team win, I was there and I did it. I was willing to do more and that paid off. I have a fantastic relationship with everybody from that team.

To me, that FAI Cup final is almost like a wedding with Cork City.

To me, that is how I felt about it. You have a good relationship, and you date for a while… you have your ups and downs. Then, at the end you say okay, are we getting married and that's it. That was the celebration.

Now I know I am linked to the city forever.

KARL SHEPPARD

Karl Sheppard celebrates following the FAI Cup final against Dundalk at the Aviva Stadium in 2017.

"

THE CUP FINAL in 2017, where we went on to win the double, that was a huge game in the Aviva Stadium. There was a lot of build up to it with me possibly joining Dundalk and all beforehand. That stands out when I think back on my time with Cork.

Going into the game, I remember we had a team meeting before the match. John Caulfield addressed the fact that I could be joining Dundalk. He addressed it in front of the group saying, 'I need to address the elephant in the room and it seems Karl will be going to Dundalk next year. But I know that I have no problem in starting him on Sunday because I know he is going to give us his all'.

So, I remember going into the game feeling very confident, just because that it was very unlike John to put the arm around the shoulder or to give me a confidence booster. Me and John would go loggerheads with each other, and we'd always be at each other. He knew he could do that with me.

So, for him to put the arm around the shoulder, it was great, and I knew I needed to go out and play well.

I knew going out into the warm-up that the cameras were going towards me. I was thinking... *this is the start of it and this was expected.* I knew that the storyline before the game was going to be about me joining Dundalk and should I be playing? At that stage, I knew that I was probably going to be staying at Cork.

But for me, I was very much focused on the fact that I am with Cork and I think that I will be staying with them next year. I knew where my loyalties stood. Going into the game I had a load of extra motivation, so it was easy to get up for the game and get ready for it.

I think I was maybe at Cork three years at that point and, for me, it was sort of the make-or-break point. The year before we won the cup, and that year going into it we had won the league. We still weren't getting a pat on the back which we felt, I suppose, that we wanted for the recognition of years of hard work... of tracking that Dundalk team, making sure we got level with them and overtook them.

It was years of hard work, not just from my own point of view, but I knew John Caulfield was working tirelessly to go and win the league and the cup. All of the backroom staff as well. Even people like Alan Bennett and Mark McNulty... to see what it meant to them.

There was that added niceness for me, having in the build-up people questioning me. To turn around and show people that they shouldn't have questioned my professionalism... all of those things combined is why that game stands out to me. I remember at the start of the 2017 season thinking it is the big games that you have to do it in, that is how you stay in the team. If you do it in the big games, you'll gain the manager's trust.

Thankfully, in that year, I played every single league game.

I remember at the start of the year having a few good games and thinking I had John's trust now, and then making sure I built on that as the year went on. He always seemed to play me at that point. It came to the tough decision then for John... *do I trust him as a person and a professional?*

Thankfully, he did.

Looking back on the game, I am obviously going to say it was the right decision because I was able to get an assist and score a peno. Thankfully, looking back, I think he made the right decision. John Caulfield's best trait is the demands he puts on people and the team. That is one hundred percent his best trait, he doesn't accept any slacking or messing whatsoever.

You have to buy into John's way of making sure that you put one hundred percent into not just how you play, but how you train. If anyone slacked up a little bit in training, whether it was in terms of their diet or their attitude in training… or even just how much they were running, they probably wouldn't be around for more than six months.

If they didn't buy in, John just made sure that they were gone, because ultimately it was all about the group and how hard we pushed each other. That is why I'd say when John set them standards, he made sure everyone did their gym work and everyone bought into how he wanted to play. So that, going into the games, they were almost easy in comparison to the standards that John put on us and that we had put on ourselves that year.

I remember in extra-time, I was absolutely shattered. I was exhausted at that moment in time and that is why I was so deep. Normally, I am never that far back collecting the ball. I remember as I passed the ball to Stephen Dooley and he had a bit of time… so, I made a second movement to get it back.

Just as I got it back, I looked up and saw Achille Campion making a bit of movement from the right hand side of the pitch across the Dundalk back four. I thought… *this pass is on here.* I don't think I've had a better assist in my career that one because of the occasion that was in it…. just to try that ball. It worked out perfectly and, thankfully, Achille was able to stick it into the back of the net.

I'd say we practiced penalties that year once a week, if not more. Everyone had to stay behind and take penalties. That is why when we went into the penalty shootout, we sort of knew who was going to be taking them.

I remember John said, 'right, who is taking them?'

It all went a bit quiet, and I think it was Stephen Dooley who said, 'Shep. you are first, aren't you.'

I was like, 'right, I am first!'

I soon as I said that… *yeah I am first…* I just got this wave of confidence that I knew I was going to score.

I remember saying to Conor McCormack and Steven Beattie that you need to take one because I knew they were big occasion people, and both took their penos well.

I remember walking up to mine.

Oddly, I had quite a poor record on penos, but I had never been as confident as that moment that I was going to score. There is probably no better way to win it. It was just great the fact that you are making memories with people in your life at that moment in time. I remember Sads (Kieran Sadlier) stepping up to take that fifth peno… and I was also very confident that he was going to score.

There was that animosity there for me between Cork City and Dundalk.

I knew I would be coming up against Dane Massey. I knew that if I got a chance to leave one in on Dane Massey, I would… and vice versa with him with me. I knew that if I went up for a header, be ready to get an elbow into the back of the head because it is that type of a game. You can play other teams in close rivalry matches and it won't be like that, but we certainly had that bit of bite between the two teams.

It was like that all around the pitch, whether it was Stephen O'Donnell, Chris Shields or Brian Gartland. Or on our side, whether it was McCormack or Beattie or Greg Bolger. We all would have been making sure that no one pulls out of a tackle going into those games. They were great games and what always made it better was the fact that the quality of football on show was always very high.

I'd always be sticking little snippets of newspapers, radio or TV clips of things that people were saying about us and trying to create that 'us against them' mentality within our group. It was something I very much believed in as a player. It was almost not trying to just motivate myself, but motivate the teammates around me.

It was always just things around Cork staggering over the line.

I think you could see that when we won it. We all came out saying we need to get a bit of respect for what we have done this year, to get a double against what people were calling the best team possibly ever to play in the League of Ireland… against that Dundalk team.

So, it was huge for us to go and win it.

We certainly did have that bit between our teeth, to say that… *yes Seánie*

Maguire was brilliant and so was Kev (O'Connor). But we still went onto beat the Dundalk team that everyone says is probably the best team ever to play in the League of Ireland. We were looking for that recognition, but look, I suppose that is life and it never really comes in the end.

Maybe a couple of years down the line, when people look back, they will say they were good times for the League of Ireland with those two teams going against each other.

In that group we just had winners throughout. Thankfully, we had a bit of experience as well. Alan Bennett and Mark McNulty were part of the previous Cork team that won the league and got to a cup final, but lost it because they were basically drinking all week. They said that they had over celebrated.

I remember John actually warning us that isn't to happen at all. 'Ye can celebrate winning the league and the cup, and it will be a much better celebration than it is just winning the cup alone,' he promised.

Or, win the league alone and then you lose the cup, and it is just then a damp squib of a celebration. He was just saying, 'let's go and have maybe one drink one night, then make sure that we train hard that week before we go into the cup final'. That we are all ready and nobody is pre-celebrating it.

Also, John used to always say, 'great, you win a cup, you win a league, but ultimately you just have to get on with it and go win the next one!'

It is when you retire that you can look back and go, 'that was great!'

It is only recently that it is starting to kick in... *okay, I am retired now, but they were great memories and great times that I had.* It is always just nice to look back on the nights out afterwards or the memories on the pitch that would come back to you every so often. You are like... *those were great times.*

For me, I had two very good spells in my career. One being when I was at Shamrock Rovers and at 19 I was starting in the Europa League. It was an unbelievable spell where I was able to get a move to the UK. For six months there, I probably played the best football of my career.

The most consistent football, however, I played was under John Caulfield. I suppose maybe across three seasons, where I felt... *now I am a big player in the League of Ireland.* Would I have wanted it to have gone on for longer... yes.

But, ultimately, I got arthritis and I didn't see that coming.

I was trying to look after my body as best as I could. It is over now, but I look back on it with very fond memories. I know things didn't end the way I would have wanted and even where the club is now, it is not where I thought the club would have been left. That is football and you live and you learn.

Cork is special in a sense that it is so big, yet it is so small. The population is huge, but you could go through the city and you'll have 10 or 15 people stop you. Whereas, if you walk through Dublin city, nobody is going to stop you, no matter how many times you walk through it.

Nobody is going to recognise you because it is so big. Cork has just such a big population who buy in to the soccer side of it. As John Caulfield would say, a big floating fan-base. Obviously, you have the diehards that are there through thick and thin. But they have a huge floating fan-base who will come in when the team is doing well. It is when I left Cork that I realised that was huge.

I think of nights when we won the double and we returned back after the FAI Cup final, we were on the stage in front of thousands of people. You probably took that for granted a bit and thought this is just normal. Then you retire and go... *they were some nights, they were brilliant.*

We were just such good friends and we had such a good dressing-room at that moment in time. Almost every day or every second day, I'd still chat to the likes of Steven Beattie or Conor McCormack. We are always chatting.

It was great that you were able to go and have such good memories with your mates. You look back on it now and just say it was a great time. It was just such a good time to do it with people in such a good dressing-room.

We had a great dressing-room. We had great craic every single day going into training. That makes it extra special, when you go and win it with a group that you actually really enjoy being around.

MORE
GREAT
SPORTS BOOKS
FROM
HERO BOOKS

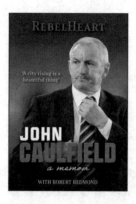

JOHN CAULFIELD
An Autobiography

JOHN CAULFIELD MIGHT have lived a whole different sporting life.

Born in the United States, in the Bronx, his family relocated to Ireland, to Roscommon – and to a GAA community. And while Caulfield loved gaelic football, his brilliance on the soccer field and his scoring touch meant that his 'football life' turned in a different direction. He would represent Roscommon and Cork on GAA fields, but it was with Cork City and in the League of Ireland that he would leave an indelible mark on the Irish sporting landscape. He won league and cup honours as a player with City. He made over 650 appearances for the club, a record, and still holds the title of the club's all-time record scorer with 197 goals. Caulfield, however, never stopped dreaming for himself and the City he adopted. In 2013, he was appointed manager of the club and he set out to bring to an end a long and fallow period for Cork supporters.

'Rebelheart' is the story of a remarkable life, and the story of Cork winning the 2016 FAI Cup, and 'the double' of League title and Cup in 2017. It is also a story of pride and ambition. And a determination to prove to a city and its people that they had every right to live their dreams on a football field.

Authors: John Caulfield with Robert Redmond

Hardback: €25.00

Paperback: €20.00

Ebook: €9.99

ISBN: 9781910827130

Buy on **Amazon**
(and paperback available in all good bookstores)

MEYLER
A Family Memoir

John and David Meyler
A story of a Father and Son
One believing in the other in Pairc Ui Chaoimh and Croke Park.
One believing in the other in the Aviva Stadium and Wembley.
A story of Wexford and Cork hurling.
A story of Cork City, and Sunderland and Hull City, and the
Republic of Ireland.
The brilliant, intimate story of the Meyler family.

Authors: John and David Meyler with Fintan O'Toole
Hardback: €25.00
Paperback: €20.00
Ebook: €9.99
ISBN: 9781910827369

Buy on **Amazon**
(and paperback available in all good bookstores)

BRIAN GARTLAND
An Autobiography

BRIAN GARTLAND WON it all in the final years of his amazing career.

He was a central part of the Dundalk team that won the Premier Division title in 2014, '15, 16, '18 and '19, and did the League and Cup 'Double' in 2015 and '18. But the Dubliner, who started out on his career with Bray Wanderers over a decade before the first of those successes, had found himself running out of time as the final leg of his football life came into sight.

He wore the colours of Bray, Shelbourne, Monaghan United and Portadown during that decade - before he got *One Last Shot* at becoming a leader in a team destined for greatness.

It might never have happened for Brian Gartland. He had *One Last Shot*... and he took it with courage, and a determination that has made him one of the outstanding footballers in League of Ireland history.

Authors: Brian Gartland with Mark McCadden
Hardback: €25.00
Paperback: €20.00
Ebook: €9.99
ISBN: 9781910827215

Buy on **Amazon**
(and paperback available in all good bookstores)

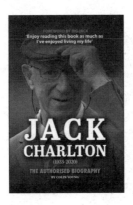

Jack Charlton
The Authorised Biography

AS ONE OF the true legends of Irish and English football, Jack Charlton was a man both loved and feared, but now the people who have lived with him all of his life introduce the real 'Big Jack' in this brilliant authorised biography which is presented in a foreword by Jack himself.

For the first time Jack's wife and family, his teammates as a World Cup winner with England in 1966, and his players during his management years with Middlesbrough, Sheffield Wednesday, Newcastle, and Ireland tell their stories of the man who dominated their lives. Graeme Souness, Chris Waddle, and Peter Beardsley amongst others, are joined by Mick McCarthy, Niall Quinn and the greatest footballers who played under Big Jack for 10 years as Ireland team boss.

This is the most personable, inviting and intimate account of Jack Charlton's life, and the book contains photographs published for the first time from Jack and Pat Charlton's personal collection.

Author: Colin Young
Hardback: €25.00
Paperback: €20.00
Ebook: €9.99
ISBN: 9781910827017

Buy on **Amazon**
(and paperback available in all good bookstores)

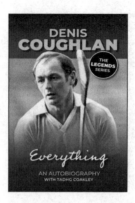

DENIS COUGHLAN
An Autobiography

DENIS COUGHLAN LIVED and played through a golden era in the GAA. And he did so brilliantly on both hurling and football fields for close on two decades.

Nobody achieved more in both codes than Cork's own Denis Coughlan, who wore the famous red with distinction for 15 years. On the field he played with and against the best, and he also enjoyed close friendships with two of the greatest GAA men of all time, Christy Ring and Jack Lynch - all three of them Glen Rovers' heroes.

With The Glen and St Nick's Denis Coughlan won it all, many times over.

At club level he won seven county, four provincial and two All-Ireland titles. And for Cork he played a central role in 10 Munster titles and five All-Irelands triumphs - four in hurling, one in football.

Four times Coughlan was also adjudged the best of the best, winning his place on All Star hurling teams. He was Hurler of the Year in 1977.

Authors: Denis Coughlan with Tadhg Coakley

Hardback: €25.00

Paperback: €20.00

Ebook: €9.99

ISBN: 9781910827161

Buy on **Amazon**
(and paperback available in all good bookstores)

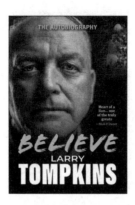

BELIEVE

Larry Tompkins: An Autobiography

HIS SELF-BELIEF WAS unbreakable. His iron will inspirational. Nothing could stop Larry Tompkins. No man, no team, as he made his football life the greatest story ever told in the long and brilliant history of the GAA.

Six years with his native Kildare left him empty-handed and heartbroken. He emigrated to New York to find a job and find a team he could lead to championship glory. In the United States, Tompkins' belief in himself never dimmed. He led Donegal to four New York championships in the Big Apple. He also found a new home for himself in Ireland and led Castlehaven to two Cork and Munster titles. In between, he also became the most valuable and feared footballer in Ireland.

BELIEVE is the story of a man who defied all the odds. In Cork's magnificent red shirt, he led his adopted county to two All-Ireland titles in 1989 and 90, one National League and six Munster titles, and he also was honoured with three All Star awards. Upon his retirement, Larry Tompkins continued to lead and inspire, and make others believe too.

Authors: Larry Tompkins with Denis Hurley

Hardback: €25.00

Paperback: €20.00

Ebook: €9.99

ISBN: 9781910827123

Buy on **Amazon**
(and paperback available in all good bookstores)

CORK LGFA
GAME OF MY LIFE

25 OF THE GREATEST CORK ladies footballers over the last 60 years remember the one game in their careers that defined their sporting lives.

Including: Juliet Murphy, Mary O'Connor, Rena Buckley, Elaine Harte, Nollaig Cleary, Bríd Stack, Norita Kelly, Geraldine O'Flynn, Martina O'Brien, Marie Ambrose, Valerie Mulcahy, Angela Walsh, Deirdre O'Reilly, Briege Corkery, Ciara O'Sullivan, Áine Terry O'Sullivan, Shauna Kelly, Orlagh Farmer, Emma Spillane, Eimear Scally, Orla Finn, Saoirse Noonan, Doireann O'Sullivan, Hannah Looney and Melissa Duggan.

A game that will live with each person forever.

Author: Ger McCarthy
Hardback: €25.00
Paperback: €20.00
Ebook: €9.99
ISBN: 9781910827499

Buy on **Amazon**
(and paperback available in all good bookstores)

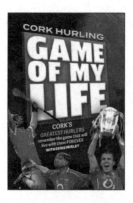

CORK HURLING
GAME OF MY LIFE

25 OF THE GREATEST CORK hurlers over the last 60 years remember the one game in their careers that defined their sporting lives.

Including: Gerald McCarthy, Tony Maher, Brian Murphy, Martin Coleman, Tom Cashman, Ger Cunningham, John Fenton, Johnny Crowley, Jimmy Barry-Murphy, John Considine, Ger Fitzgerald, Tony O'Sullivan, Tomás Mulcahy, Seán O'Gorman, Denis Walsh, Seánie McGrath, Ronan Curran, Wayne Sherlock, Kieran Murphy, Tom Kenny, Shane O'Neill, Ben O'Connor, Stephen McDonnell, Anthony Nash and Daniel Kearney.

A game that will live with each person forever.

Author: Denis Hurley
Hardback: €25.00
Paperback: €20.00
Ebook: €9.99
ISBN: 9781910827451

Buy on **Amazon**
(and paperback available in all good bookstores)